# SKETCHING GUANTANAMO

# SKETCHING GUANTANAMO

Court Sketches of the Military Tribunals, 2006-2013

JANET HAMLIN

FANTAGRAPHICS BOOKS

# TABLE OF CONTENTS

# ~~FOREWORD~~

by Carol Rosenberg

TO DRAW SOME OF THE MOST DAMNED PEOPLE ON EARTH, JANET HAMLIN HAS LUGGED HER CHARCOALS AND SKETCHPAD INSIDE A CRAMMED PENTAGON CARGO PLANE.

She has been reproached by the man accused of masterminding 9/11 for drawing his nose too large. She has been used as a centerpiece for Guantanamo stagecraft — the Pentagon's perp walk of press to portray the court proceedings as transparent. And she's been made to camp out inside a makeshift tent city when it inconvenienced her military hosts to house her in the hotels that dot the uniquely American base in southeast Cuba. In short, Janet Hamlin has worked as a sketch artist like no other in an American court like no other: at the Defense Department's Military Commissions, the tribunal chambers at Guantanamo Bay. And, as this collection illustrates, she has done it with integrity and grace, despite the tradeoffs she's made for a front-row seat to this chapter of American history.

Take a look at the young Canadian who grew into manhood behind the barbed wire of Guantanamo — beard and all — claiming his innocence, and that he was tortured, until he ultimately confessed to committing a war crime when he was 15.

Then peer through double-glazed soundproof glass as Hamlin gives the world its first look at the man who boasted that he orchestrated the 9/11 mass murder. Khalid Sheik Mohammed disappeared into the CIA's dark sites to 183 rounds of waterboarding, last seen in a tattered T-shirt in need of a shave. Next he emerges on her sketchpad — a gray-bearded figure at the Guantanamo war court, who was granted the Pentagon's prerogative of wielding a censor's pen. One morning in 2006, Hamlin put a fluorescent orange charcoal to her pad to capture the defiance of an Ethiopian captive who came to court in a traditional Muslim tunic — specially dyed in a shop in London to match the jumpsuit of the condemned.

That man, Binyam Mohamed, is gone from Guantanamo now: set free by diplomatic dealings begun during the George W. Bush administration even as prosecutors accused him of un-hatched plots. But the sketch artist's work endures, an exclusive look inside a courtroom walled off from the world by a White House that fused American criminal law and military justice — an evolving experiment that continues to this day.

Like the detainees themselves, Hamlin got to Guantanamo because of what Bush saw as a new kind of warfare, and a new kind of response. Journalists were allowed into Guantanamo from the very start, in January 2002, to show America, still reeling from the September 11 attacks, that its military was fighting back. But this transparency went only so far. Fearful of an enemy still at large, the captives' identities were kept secret as the United States interrogated them for leads to sleeper cells and the al-Qaida leadership. The architects of Guantanamo explained it like this: The Geneva Conventions forbid the parade of prisoners as humiliation. Thus cameramen were instructed to photograph the detainees at a distance to make them unrecognizable, even to their mothers, or to photograph the men from behind, or from the neck down.

Flash-forward nearly three years, when the Pentagon established the Military Commissions, the hilltop tribunals for captives suspected of being not only "enemy combatants," but war criminals too. The Bush administration wanted to show the world that it was getting a measure of justice. It cast these captives as suicidal, fanatical terrorists.

Osama bin Laden was still at large, and the alleged 9/11 architects were out of the reach of Military Commission justice, in CIA custody. The first charges brought far more mundane foot soldiers to the dock — bin Laden's driver, an al-Qaida publicist, and a child soldier whose family had celebrated feast holidays with bin Laden.

The dilemma was how much of these men to show to the world. At first, the Pentagon insisted that the sketch artist draw the accused as eerie, ghost-like, otherworldly people — by blurring their features, or drawing them from behind.

In this collection, you will see those images. But with time, the men's features are filled in; their identities come into focus, because the media pushed back against the restrictions at Guantanamo.

In federal courts and military courts-martial, a sketch artist can bring the tools of the trade to court — a good night's sleep, binoculars, a charcoal sharpener, and an artist's imagination — to show a courtroom where photographers cannot go. Not so at Guantanamo.

To report the news, Hamlin and the journalists, at first, got officers' guest quarters. You can see the traces of these courtesies in her charcoal sketches of life beyond the court. Now the media is confined to "Camp Justice." Reporters airlifted to the war court by the Pentagon work out of a filing center in a long-ago abandoned airport hangar, sleep inside canvas tents powered by screeching generators so inhospitable that the enlisted troops assigned to keep watch on the media refused to stay there. Soldiers and sailors come and go in shifts, like guards at the detention center, rather than spend an extra moment at the Hollywood-style stage set where the military chills reporters' drinking water in a portable morgue meant to fly the dead home from war.

Like the photojournalists, Hamlin must submit to invasive censorship of her images, conditions once unimaginable in Western democracy. A court security officer can instruct her to smudge a captive's features to render him less life-like. This did happen. A judge can forbid her to draw the jury, even in silhouette, unperturbed by the image of imperiousness. This happened too. At Guantanamo, an accused arch-terrorist can inspect a sketch drawn in the spectators' gallery and order the artist to refashion his nose.

In no other American court must you agree to 24-hour military custody, to have escorts eavesdrop on your calls home to wish your daughter good night, to have a Pentagon security officer glue an APPROVED sticker on your drawing before you disseminate it.

It is a stark contrast to the images that emerged from Nuremberg in the aftermath of World War II. Google the city where the West brought the Nazis to justice, and you can see a photograph of the German military commander Hermann Göring in the dock, MPs standing behind him. Search for the al-Qaida operations chief Khalid Sheik Mohammed in court, and you get Janet Hamlin's sketches.

For Janet Hamlin, the price of access to the proceedings has been a walk to court surrounded by a phalanx of forces, strutting for souvenir photographs they can post on Facebook. For the Pentagon, the pictures illustrate war court transparency: See the sketch artist's battlefield access to the distant base. Out of camera sight are the sailors' swimming pools, playgrounds, fast food counters.

Yet throughout it all, the artist among the journalists has retained her optimism and an eager eye, seeking to chip away at the constraints. Perhaps this time a military judge will take a page from the federal courts and permit the artist to sit closer to the accused, a better vantage point. Perhaps the guards will stop the endless searches of this returning artist.

For eight years, Janet Hamlin has joined a small band of journalists dedicated to the unenviable duty of reporting from a place like nowhere else. This collection lets you look inside. ★

*Miami Herald reporter Carol Rosenberg has covered the Middle East, terror, and, for more than a decade, Guantanamo, where she's been dubbed by colleagues and colonels "The Dean of the Military Commissions Press Corps." She has been awarded the Robert F. Kennedy Domestic Print journalism prize for her coverage of Guantanamo, as well as multiple awards by the Society of Professional Journalists.*

# ~~PRELUDE~~

by Janet Hamlin

Sept. 11, 2001. The skies had darkened, and a silent fluttering filled the air as papers floated down on my Brooklyn steps. The edges were burned, and tiny holes pocked the pages of stock reports; a three-page health file; a document from Cantor Fitzgerald. The streets below were no longer filled with wailing vehicles. People walked past, cupping their hands or handkerchiefs over their faces against the thick, acrid air. You did not want to be out in it unless you had to. The towers I used to see from my window, gone forever.

Five years later: Art Director Scott Johnson at the Associated Press sent me to sketch a young Canadian detainee named Omar Khadr at Guantanamo, then Australian David Hicks in 2007, and again the still-teenage Khadr later that same year.

In June 2008, CNN hired me as a freelancer to draw the arraignment of the 9/11 accused: a first-ever view of the confessed mastermind Khalid Sheikh Mohammed, along with the four other men to be charged as alleged co-conspirators.

I still go to Guantanamo as a freelance pool artist on assignment, sketching, photographing, and documenting everything I've seen and experienced at the place everybody down there calls "Gitmo," both inside and outside the courts. ★

OPPOSITE: The new World Trade Center, under construction in May 2012. The light flare is eerily reminiscent of the lights beamed every 9/11 as a tribute to the victims.

TOP: This page is a document that fell near the front of my house on Sept. 11, 2001.

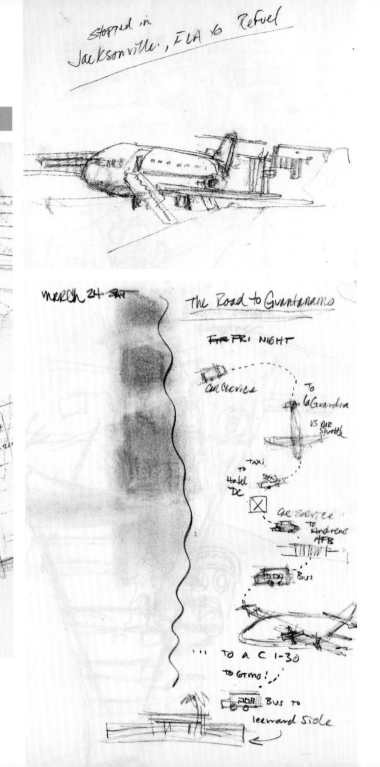

# Getting There

I've taken a variety of transport — planes, trains, automobiles — to get to Andrews Air Force Base in Maryland, the media's gateway to Guantanamo. And that's when it starts to get interesting. Depending on which charter the Pentagon gets, to reach Gitmo, I've sat for hours in lumbering C130 cargo planes; other times, I've watched movies and been served breakfasts in 737 jets. Landing there puts you on one side of the bay in southeast Cuba. Next, there's a bus to a ferryboat and 30-minute ride to reach the war court complex on the main base section of Guantanamo, Windward side, where we live and work in the compound the Pentagon calls "Camp Justice." It's built atop an old runway: McCalla Field. Camp Justice consists of portable units for some Commissions staff, the Expeditionary Legal Complex, and McCalla Hangar. (Just recently, guarded gates were put in so that during commissions you cannot enter or exit the compound without proper ID.) We sleep in a tent city and work inside the abandoned McCalla Hangar, which was once used for blimps. It has office space with $150-a-week Internet and little interior buildings where the military holds press conferences and conducts what it calls Operational Security Reviews, a kind of censorship known as OpSec. OpSec reviews all photos and videos, deleting those that show prohibited views they have determined threaten security and privacy. We are given a list of "no shoot" items in a pre-press conference, along with ground rules beforehand.

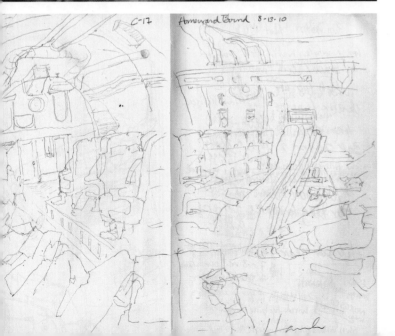

C-17    Homeward Bound 8-13-10

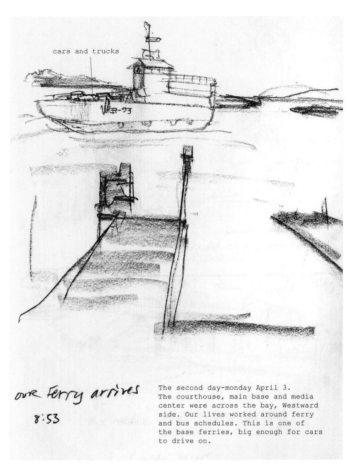

our ferry arrives
8:53

The second day-monday April 3.
The courthouse, main base and media
center were across the bay, Westward
side. Our lives worked around ferry
and bus schedules. This is one of
the base ferries, big enough for cars
to drive on.

LEFT, TOP: Sketching what was outside the window of our chartered plane as we ramp up to depart Andrews Air Force Base, Md. for Gitmo.

LEFT, CENTER: On this trip home, I hitched an available flight out a day early on a plane filled with new generals. I've never seen a fitter group of middle-aged people in my life. We were asked to not speak to them unless spoken to, due to their newly minted rank, and because they had nothing to do with the trials. I sat on the side seats with a few media people who had also opted to fly home early. This was a C-17, bigger and more modern than the C-130.

RIGHT: Upon landing, we take a ferry to the main portion of the base on the Windward side. That's where we live and work out of Camp Justice, our tent city built on an old runway near the courts. Internet and workrooms have been constructed in an old airplane hangar.

13

I've flown in the C-130 several times to get to Gitmo. It's a workhorse of a plane, a propeller-driven "flying garage" with a ramp that comes down in the back wide enough to drive a vehicle inside. We sit on mesh netting with canvas seats, and over-the-shoulder straps for seatbelts. It's so loud inside you need to wear earplugs and gesture, shout, or write to communicate. Recently, though, we've been consolidated onto charter planes, often riding with family members of victims and court personnel.

# A Court Like No Other

Guantanamo tribunals differed from the other court drawing I've done. For instance, there were faces I was not allowed to draw, and each drawing could not leave the courtroom until a Pentagon official reviewed it. He would examine the art, occasionally have me erase some of the details, then sign and stamp the art once approved. Then I carried the sketches back, uploaded them to the media pool with descriptions, grabbed lunch, and got back for the afternoon session, going through three levels of security every time we entered or left the court area, always with an escort. Time is precious.

For court sketching, I use brown-toned paper and pastels. The brown tones cut down on the time it takes to "fill in" the drawing. I build out the darks and lights from the middle brown tones. Pastels allow me to work over what I've drawn should a person move and details change; such as the time Khalid Sheikh Mohammed was sitting down, but abruptly stood up to address the judge — a powerful image, so I quickly drew over what I'd drawn, moving the others down so they were seated below him. Pastels allow you to do that.

My drawings are a sort of "visual journalism"; I must edit out some things that are superfluous, and focus on the elements that are most important, at times outlining or enlarging things of importance to help tell the story in the best way possible, without skewing or fictionalizing the scene. Rarely do I have an unobstructed view. Usually, there are people between what I'm drawing and me: as well as poles, desks, etc. I work to create a composition that focuses on the scene overall while omitting all the

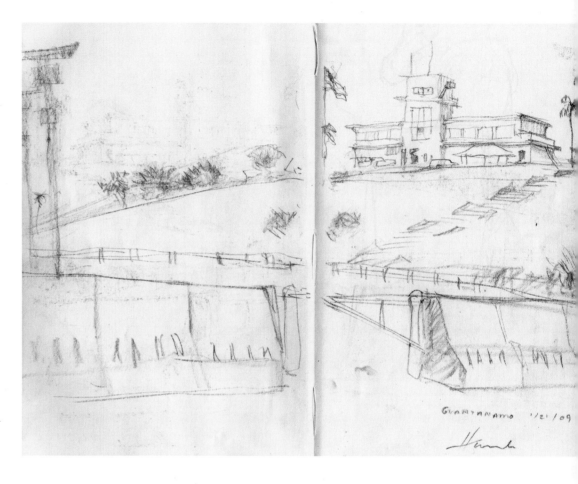

unnecessary or obstructive elements. I am really conscious of keeping things as true as possible.

Time is of the essence. While I want every drawing to be well composed, sometimes I just don't have time to finish a scene I had in mind. A new witness is called, or something may happen that demands a new drawing. Often my supplies are stacked on

my board, which can cause an empty space. Not knowing how long I have, I get what I can as quickly as possible while the subjects are in constant motion. Evidence shown on a screen in court is often not released. So I sketch that too, sometimes in a separate vignette.

Because Guantanamo is unique, every picture tells a story but has a backstory.

TOP: Human rights lawyers, defense, and prosecution hold impromptu meetings with the press just outside the hangar workspace. At the drop of a hat, the journalists need to stop what they are doing, grab their notebooks, pens, and recorders, and cover these meetings. Our work hours become seamless, endless days.

A small building was built for these meetings, but we only use it as designated for scheduled, formal press conferences or briefings.

BOTTOM: A video feed of the proceedings is piped over to the media center so people can follow outside the court. No photography or videotaping of the footage is allowed, as posted signs warn. Anything shot that is not approved is deleted or scrubbed from hard drives.

OVERLEAF: Sometimes I like to sketch the spectator's gallery. For one, the people can be interesting. Of equal importance is that it shows more of what goes on at the court. Reporters who get to observe are chosen by lottery; in this instance, just seven spaces were set aside. Those are human rights lawyers, sitting separately, in the second row.

KHADR 4/2006 Caryl Rosenberg

# BINYAM MOHAMED

Though I was sent to Guantanamo to draw Omar Khadr, I would sketch as many other hearings as I could. This was such a rare opportunity that I didn't want to miss a chance to draw. And so I went up to the court to sketch Binyam Mohamed, accused of plotting to blow up apartment buildings and gas stations in the United States. Omar Khadr had worn civilian clothes, so it was expected that Mohamed would too. He did, but his traditional tunic was specially dyed orange, like the prison jumpsuits that had become a negative symbol of Guantanamo. A murmur rippled through the courtroom. I reached for my orange charcoal and a day of drama ensued. Mohamed's military lawyer refused to speak on his behalf, because the accused wanted to represent himself. That angered the judge, who ordered the defender on her feet, and to speak. There was a standoff when she refused his order and invoked the Fifth Amendment.

The judge called a break, and upon reconsideration decided that Mohamed could speak for himself. When Mohamed did, he declared the tribunals "a con" and held up a sign that said "Conn," a play on Commission and Conn-mission. Court rules at the time required that I blur Mohamed's facial features, so I drew the scene rather than focus in.

Mohamed went on a hunger strike in February 2009; shortly after, charges were dropped, and Mohamed was released.

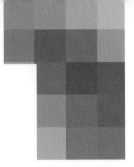

# ~~DAVID HICKS~~

by Jane Sutton, Reuters Correspondent

## AUSTRALIAN PRISONER DAVID HICKS WAS INITIALLY PORTRAYED BY THE U.S. MILITARY AS ONE OF GUANTANAMO'S MOST DANGEROUS DETAINEES.

After five years in captivity, the former cowboy and kangaroo skinner pleaded guilty in 2007 to providing material support for terrorism and became the first convict in the U.S. war crimes tribunals at Guantanamo.

As part of a plea deal that limited his sentence to nine months, he admitted that he trained at al-Qaida camps in Afghanistan but said he fled his first battle, sold his gun to raise cab fare, and was captured by the U.S.-backed Northern Alliance as he tried to escape into Pakistan.

Hicks was allowed to serve most of his sentence back home in Australia. After he was freed, he wrote a book saying he was innocent and had signed the plea deal under duress because he believed it was the only way out of Guantanamo. He said his training in Afghanistan was for military purposes, not terrorism.

The Australian government tried to block him from receiving any of the modest proceeds from the book, under a law that prevents convicts from profiting from their crimes. They gave up after Hicks' lawyers showed evidence that Hicks had been beaten and subjected to sleep deprivation and other harsh conditions of confinement before signing the plea deal.

In 2012, a U.S. appeals court in Washington ruled in the case of another Guantanamo convict, Osama bin Laden's one-time driver and bodyguard Salim Hamdan, that providing material support for terrorism was not a war crime during the time Hamdan and Hicks were accused of aiding al-Qaida in Afghanistan in 2001. They were prosecuted under a U.S. law enacted in 2006, and the court said it could not be applied retroactively.

The ruling overturned Hamdan's conviction. Although Hicks waived his right to appeal when he pleaded guilty at Guantanamo, his lawyers said the ruling laid the groundwork for his conviction to be thrown out as well. ★

*Jane Sutton is a journalist with the Thomson Reuters news agency who has been covering the Guantanamo detention operation since January 2002.*

Hicks    Hamlin  4/2007

4/2007 HICKS

FIRST RELEASED DRAWING OF A DETAINEE'S FACE

# The Breakthrough: Sketching Facial Features

I returned to sketch David Hicks in March 2007. Hicks is an Australian who eventually admitted that he trained at al-Qaida camps in Afghanistan. No one had seen what he looked like for six years. I had been told that I might be able to draw his face this time, rather than have to smudge it, which was a huge deal. But when I got into court, the seat I'd requested was taken, and I found myself seated *behind* him. All I could see was the back of Hicks, and he'd changed radically — from a fit militant to an un-groomed, longhaired, pasty prisoner. His explanation was that he had grown out his hair to drape over his eyes and sleep. The guards always left the lights on, he said.

At the break, I called an official over, and requested to move to a now-vacated seat that offered a view of the man I'd come to court to draw. Request denied. I asked to speak directly with the court officer. Clearly agitated, she came over. I fervently explained my position. The answer was still no. "Okay, then I might as well leave," I replied. "I can't do the job I was sent to do." I was serious. And desperate. Let them explain to the media why their artist couldn't get a decent sketch. She conceded, but I had to draw with my supplies in my lap and lose the table I had earlier.

This first drawing of his face — actually, the first drawing of *any* detainee's face — went out before being reviewed and affixed with a sticker. My military escort at that moment cleared it, and said it didn't have to wait for an official "APPROVED" stamp. So I rolled it up and handed it off to NPR journalist Jackie Northam, who carried it to waiting

OPPOSITE: David Hicks pleaded guilty, which was completely unexpected, so the trial suddenly moved forward.

LEFT: Three days later Hicks' appearance changed dramatically. He got a haircut and a suit.

media people. The image was out in no time, but not without drama. I was severely reprimanded and found myself sitting sandwiched between guards the rest of the day. Thankfully, plenty of people witnessed the escort saying it was okay, so I was not held accountable. Once out, there was no turning back, and I was able to draw faces of detainees in court from then on. To me, even with a positive outcome, the episode was a stressful one. The last thing I wanted was to erode any trust I had built up with the military.

The Associated Press bestowed on me a coveted "Beat of the Week" award, the first given to an artist rather than a writer or photographer.

22

RIGHT: For the first time since the start of the commissions, a military jury was selected. Officers from the different U.S. services were flown in. As is the case with any jury, I can't draw their faces, but I can show uniforms, skin tone, and gender.

OPPOSITE: Hicks pleaded guilty and a military jury gave him the maximum sentence: seven years in this case. The judge thanked them for their service and excused them. Once they were gone, the judge announced that a pre-set plea deal trumped the sentence. Hicks was soon sent home to Australia to serve just nine more months in jail there. He is now free, married, and has written a book.

4/2007  HICKS PLEADS GUILTY

# ~~OMAR KHADAR~~

by Michelle Shephard

KHADR 6/·/09

Hardin

Detainee ISN 766 was one of the youngest captives to be held at Guantanamo Bay: shot and captured at the age of 15 following a lengthy July 2002 firefight that killed U.S. Delta Force Sgt. First Class Christopher J. Speer.

The story of Canadian Omar Khadr is one of the more famous Gitmo tales and one that divided the public.

Civil rights advocates said Khadr's case exemplified how the U.S. administration had lost the moral high ground after 9/11 and flouted international law by prosecuting a child soldier.

Some saw Khadr as a victim himself, only in Afghanistan at the behest of his father — an associate of Osama bin Laden who was killed by Pakistani forces a year after Khadr's capture. Pentagon lawyers told Guantanamo's military commission that a grievously wounded Khadr was interrogated in the U.S. prison in Bagram before his transfer to Gitmo, sometimes brought into sessions sedated and on a stretcher. His chief interrogator was later convicted for his role in the death of another Bagram detainee — an innocent Afghan taxi driver.

Others saw Khadr as an unrepentant terrorist and murderer and claimed his fate was not severe enough for taking the life of Speer and injuring others. In Canada, Khadr's family loomed large over the case. His mother and sister had publicly praised the fight in

Afghanistan and condemned Canada's liberal laws. They were largely despised for their former support of al-Qaida and viewed as "Canadians of convenience."

Khadr's case began in 2002 under the Bush administration, and went to trial eight years later under Obama's. In October 2010, a 24-year-old Khadr pleaded guilty to the five war crimes in return for an eight-year sentence. He was transferred to Canadian custody in September 2012 to serve the remainder of his sentence. Janet Hamlin provided the only glimpse of Khadr with remarkable likeness, documenting his adolescence from that first public appearance in 2006, when he stood before a military judge as a pimply and defiant teenager. Her sketches were the official record of the famous Detainee 766, and Hamlin didn't miss an appearance. For many of his pre-trial appearances, she captured his hunched pose as he concentrated on his own sketches, bored with the legalese. Sometimes, Khadr would crane his neck to try to see what Hamlin was doing.

Hamlin was there in the fall of 2010 to capture the last time Khadr appeared before a military commission, pleading guilty as Speer's widow Tabitha sat in the front row, clutching photos of her children.

He left the court that day no longer 766, but as a convicted war criminal — the youngest one in modern day history. ★

*Michelle Shephard is an award-winning national security correspondent for the* Toronto Star, *Canada's largest newspaper. She is the three-time recipient of the National Newspaper Award — Canada's top newspaper prize — and the Governor General's Michener Award for Public Service Journalism. She was an associate producer of the Oscar-nominated documentary* Under Fire: Journalists in Combat *and is producing a documentary on the Uighur detainees from Guantanamo. Shephard has authored two books:* Guantanamo's Child: The Untold Story of Omar Khadr *and* Decade of Fear: Reporting from Terrorism's Grey Zone.

25

TOP: April of 2006. Khadr kept looking at himself on a monitor that showed the courtroom scene from security cameras. So I sketched that detail in as well, though a bit nervously. I was not allowed to draw his features, so I had to be prepared to erase anything that was too detailed. Addressing the judge is Marine Lt. Col. Colby Vokey, his defense attorney. Vokey was very frustrated and at one point pounded his fist on the table during a clash about rules for the proceedings.

BOTTOM: Omar Khadr, June 4, 2007. The Canadian got a new defense team: Navy Lt. Cmdr. William C. Kuebler and Canadian lawyers Dennis Edney and Nathan Whitling. This time Omar Khadr appeared unkempt, with shaggy hair and a khaki-colored prison uniform, symbolizing mild non-compliance.

TOP LEFT May 8, 2008. Omar Khadr's hearings were moving forward, and I was sent to sketch. This time he wore a white uniform, signifying he was cooperative in his confinement.

TOP RIGHT: Because of Khadr's status as the only Canadian, and also a minor, the media was greatly interested in every procedure. As a result, I have a visual record of the entire process over the course of four years.

Omar Khadr's hearings were moving forward with a new legal team; his assigned primary defense lawyer was Navy Lt. Cmdr. William Kuebler, sitting at the far right of the table.

I was also given more freedom to move about the court and sketch from different vantage points.

BOTTOM LEFT: Dec. 8, 2008. Omar Khadr was sitting with his defense team during a hearing while a witness, identified only as Interrogator Number 11, testified. Here I was instructed to omit her features to preserve her anonymity.

BOTTOM RIGHT: Dec. 12, 2008. That day's motions to produce photographic evidence were denied. His defense team suggested that the photos might cast doubt on the claim that he had thrown a lethal grenade.

TOP: Jan. 19, 2009. A close-up sketch of Omar Khadr while prosecutors screened a video showing him making a bomb as a young teen. The video was recovered at the compound where Khadr was captured, nearly dead.

BOTTOM: Jan. 20, 2009. Omar Khadr with his defense team during a pre-trial hearing. FBI agent Robert Fuller was testifying that he interrogated Khadr on his ties to al-Qaida. This is a good example of my visual editing: My view was obscured by a white column between prosecution and defense that blocked my view of a lot of detail. To compensate, I'd lean far right and far left to fill in the scene.

TOP LEFT: Omar Khadr during a hearing on April 8, 2009. Navy Lt. Cmdr. William Kuebler was arguing that Khadr was a "child soldier" and victim of al-Qaida, not a member, whose charges should be dismissed.

This would be Kuebler's final day in court representing Khadr.

TOP RIGHT: June 1, 2009. Canadian defendant Omar Khadr during a hearing inside Courtroom 1, where there was disharmony among his defense team. At his right was Michel Paradis, a Pentagon-paid civilian defense lawyer; a Navy paralegal; and Navy Lt. Cmdr. William Kuebler and Navy Cmdr. Walter Ruiz, both defense attorneys. Khadr asked the judge in the case to dismiss all his U.S. military defense attorneys Monday, saying he had lost trust in the lawyers after seeing them argue among themselves.

BOTTOM LEFT: An agent testified about a video that was found at the compound where Khadr was captured. On the video, a 14-year-old Khadr was seen learning how to assemble bombs. He reluctantly came to court, his damaged eye apparently bothering him, so you can see him here with his head in his hands. The agent holds a disk of the movie.

BOTTOM RIGHT: One constant figure in Omar Khadr's defense was Canadian civilian attorney Dennis Edney, on the right here. He served as Foreign Attorney Consultant to the defense team.

CPT. BRUZZESE

Here Marine Corps Capt. Laura Bruzzese explains an hour-long delay. According to Spencer Ackerman's April 29, 2010 Washington Independent report, when Capt. Bruzzese went to go collect Omar Khadr for a pre-trial hearing, "Khadr had a blanket over his head and complained of pain in his left eye … She had him escorted to the infirmary, where he received an eyedrop for the pain, and in Camp Delta security officers attempted to load Khadr into a van to transport him to court. Part of that transfer involved putting what is called 'Eyes and Ears' on Khadr: blackout ski goggles and earmuffs to block out his senses while in transit."

He showed up covering his eyes, clearly upset.

TOP LEFT: April 30, 2010. Omar Khadr's case was progressing. Witnesses were being called during pre-trial discovery hearings. This was a longer trip than most, with multiple witnesses. After missing Hamdan's trial finale, I vowed to cover the Khadr case from start to finish. Here we see Naval Criminal Investigative Service (NCIS) agent Jocelyn Dillard telling Air Force Capt. Christopher Eason, a case prosecutor, that Omar Khadr cooperated during interrogation. The agent requested that I smudge her features before the drawing was released, so that while her name was known, her face would not be.

TOP RIGHT: May 1, 2010. Yet another new lawyer arrived at Guantanamo to work for Omar Khadr. Here, Washington D.C. attorney Kobie Flowers was questioning a witness during a pre-trial hearing.

BOTTOM LEFT: A prosecutor questions a pretty interrogator — known as Interrogator Number 11 — about her claim that she gained Omar Khadr's trust by acting as a "mother figure." Khadr's latest defense lawyer, Army Lt. Col. Jon Jackson, is in the foreground. Khadr had chosen to boycott the hearing for a few days, claiming he distrusted the system.

BOTTOM RIGHT: A prosecutor questioning an agent during a pre-trial hearing.

TOP LEFT: May 1, 2010. Khadr's other Washington, D.C. defense attorney, Barry Coburn, questioned an Army officer who testified by video-feed as Lt. Col. "W."

People testifying with a pseudonym had to have their facial features blurred to ensure their anonymity.

TOP RIGHT: Air Force Capt. Christopher Eason, a prosecutor, questioned FBI agent Larry Girod, one of Omar Khadr's interrogators. Girod described Khadr several times as quiet, cooperative, and respectful, but said he never showed any regret about his actions, spoke in a "cold and callous" manner at times, and "appeared to be boasting." Khadr's lawyers countered that Girod appeared to be "editorializing" about Khadr's state of mind.

BOTTOM LEFT: Defense lawyer Barry Coburn questioned FBI agent Doug Raubal in the Omar Khadr Military Commission hearings. FBI agent Doug Raubal, an eight-year FBI Joint Terrorism Task Force veteran, testified he'd never heard of the Rumsfeld Memos.

BOTTOM RIGHT: May 3, 2010. Omar Khadr was in court after several days' absence. You can see the process I use to build my drawings: using dark brown, then bringing in lights, darks, and colors to refine and pull out details once I have the scene in place. Focusing on the primary person, I build out from there. Sometimes things move so fast in court I have to abandon the sketch and move on. That's what I did here.

31

TOP: May 3, 2010. Witness NCIS agent Greg Finley, via video telecast, testified that he interrogated Khadr about 20 times. Omar Khadr told him he believed he was a terrorist trained by al-Qaida and that he wanted to benefit from bounties offered for each American killed.

BOTTOM: A former U.S. combat medic testified — as "Mr. M." — that he saw Omar Khadr chained to a door by his wrists, with his arms just above eye level, during his detention in Bagram, Afghanistan, with a hood over his head. When he lifted the hood, he saw Khadr weeping.

LEFT: May 5, 2010. Retired Army Reserves Col. Marjorie Mosier, an ophthalmologist who was flown in to Afghanistan to operate on Omar Khadr in Bagram, testified that she was able to remove shrapnel and debris from his eyes and save the vision in one eye. She described using larger instruments than usual, because that's what was available on short notice.

TOP RIGHT: An Army master sergeant, "Interrogator Number 2," anonymously testified that he observed other troops implement a range of techniques, including "fear down" to reduce anxiety and "fear of incarceration" — the threat of longer detention if he didn't cooperate — to interrogate Omar Khadr.

BOTTOM RIGHT: Air Force Capt. Christopher Eason, a prosecutor, questioned Army Col. Donna Hershey, a nurse who ran the hospital at Bagram Air Force base in 2002 when the military brought a severely wounded Omar Khadr in for treatment a day after his capture in a firefight. She testified that no one interrogated Khadr while he was there getting treatment, though some tried. A diagram of the hospital can be seen on the monitor behind her.

TOP: May 4, 2010. Army Lt. Col. Jon Jackson, Omar Khadr's defense lawyer, questioned an interrogator wearing the uniform of an Army master sergeant at a hearing. At the trial, the public knew him only as "Interrogator Number 2." Here, Jackson demonstrates how Khadr was shackled and gets confirmation from the interrogator, who also said the young captive looked fatigued.

BOTTOM: FBI agent Tim Fehmel testified via video link. The witnesses that spoke during pre-trial hearings helped build both the defense's and the prosecution's cases. The pace in which they came and went kept me on my toes. I was determined to capture every detail I could, even when it seemed mundane — such as the subject's background on the video monitor; for me, the goal was to bring out as much true visual information as possible.

OPPOSITE: One thing I wanted to show was Omar Khadr's damaged left eye, seen on the right side of his face here. I couldn't see it very easily from where I was sitting in court. So I drew it from a nearby monitor. Khadr would flex his wrists and write or draw during the sessions.

34

TOP LEFT: Wednesday, May 5, 2010. Air Force Capt. Christopher Eason questioned head and neck surgeon Army Col. James Post. Post was commander of Bagram Hospital when Khadr was there. Post testified that Khadr wasn't interrogated at the hospital, even though Khadr's affidavit claimed he was. Screenings are not considered interrogations.

TOP RIGHT: Defense council Kobie Flowers questioned "Interrogator Number 17" via video link. This interrogator had worked in the Bagram detention facility while Omar Khadr was held there and had interacted with him, although never took part in his actual interrogations. He described Khadr as a "young man who never had a chance to grow up."

BOTTOM LEFT: Khadr listens while a former guard, nicknamed "The Monster," recalls how he felt sympathy for the young detainee.

BOTTOM RIGHT: May 6, 2010. "Interrogator Number 1," identified elsewhere as former Army Sgt. Joshua Claus, testified, via video link, as one of Khadr's first interrogators. Claus' testimony took on greater significance because he had been sentenced to five months in prison for assault, prisoner maltreatment, and lying to investigators in a different Bagram case. Claus was granted immunity from prosecution for any possible abuse of Khadr in exchange for testifying here.

36

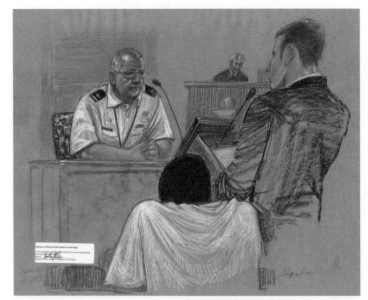

INTERROGATOR #1

May 6, 2010. On the final day of two weeks of testimony, after the court session had ended, the military summoned some reporters. Reading from a letter, our military escort announced that four seasoned journalists would be forbidden to return to Guantanamo for reporting the name of "Interrogator Number 1," even though he had given his name, Joshua Claus, during an interview that was published years earlier with the *Toronto Star*'s Michelle Shephard. Claus told Shephard that he had agreed to the interview "to clear my name." The journalists were: Michelle Shephard, Stephen Edwards of the Canwest News Service, Paul Koring of *The Globe and Mail*, and Carol Rosenberg of *The Miami Herald*. It was a stunning announcement, and the mood in the media workroom was melancholy.

Some of the journalists hired First Amendment lawyer David Schulz, who appealed the ban as unconstitutional. He argued for greater transparency on behalf of more than a dozen news organizations, including public and press access to the to U.S. viewing sites, where currently only victims can watch. Judge Army Col. James Pohl rejected his motion, but a few months later, the Pentagon relented and rescinded the ban. The Defense Department's top lawyer, Jeh C. Johnson, had facilitated the reporters' reinstatement, and the rules that governed media access to the commissions began to be rewritten.

Defense lawyer Barry Coburn questioned "Interrogator Number 1" about how Omar Khadr was shackled during interrogation. In the foreground, you can see how Khadr held his head down and covered his eyes.

37

TOP LEFT: Aug. 9, 2010. After eight years in detention and firing three sets of lawyers, the trial of Omar Khadr is set to begin. Here, Khadr is speaking with his Canadian lawyer Dennis Edney.

TOP RIGHT: Army Lt. Col. Jon Jackson, Omar Khadr's military-assigned lawyer, remained on the case. The judge would not allow Khadr to fire him, so the primary task of defending the Canadian at trial fell on his shoulders.

BOTTOM: Omar Khadr got upset as they showed video of four soldiers wearing blue latex gloves trying to examine him. He was non-cooperative and upset in the video.

OPPOSITE: Khadr watched as jury selection began, wearing a suit for the first time. On this day, to signal start of the actual trial, he entered not-guilty pleas to the five changes he faced.

KHADR    8-10-10

39

This was the only drawing I did that shows the jury. Even though I'd sketched three trials with juries in Guantanamo, this judge, Army Col. Patrick Parrish, ordered that I could not draw any members of the jury — even as outlines. I was reprimanded for doing this sketch, and from then on had to draw symbols to show the jury. At the same time in a nearby court where Ibrahim al Qosi was being sentenced, I was permitted to sketch the jury in detail.

In this court, the rules were different. The jury pool was made up of military officers, whose identities were shielded under court order. Five needed to be selected for a jury. When asked whether they believed it fair to try a 15-year-old as an adult, all said they did in this case.

8-10-10 MORNING
ONLY DRAWING OF JURY- ORDERED
TO NOT DRAW THEM THEREAFTER
BY JUDGE'S protective
order

TOP: Prosecution lawyer Jeff Groharing asks a potential member of the jury if he or she can remain impartial during jury selection.

BOTTOM: Khadr is speaking with his Canadian lawyer Dennis Edney.

41

OPPOSITE: Dr. Michael Welner, a forensic psychiatrist hired to assess Omar Khadr, testified for the prosecution. He said Khadr had "been marinating in a radical jihadist community" and that Khadr could not be rehabilitated. The defense countered that Welner's assessments were based primarily on the controversial work of a third-party psychiatrist, rather than his direct assessment of Khadr, in an effort to discredit him.

TOP: A Special Forces commander, "Army Col. W," who led the July 27, 2002 assault hours later wrote a report that said the combatant who threw the grenade was dead — presumably ruling out Khadr.

He told the court that he had always believed Khadr was the culprit, but assumed he had died because he was found gravely wounded in the rubble of the compound where he was captured. "Col. W" wrote in a subsequent after-action report that the combatant who killed Army Sergeant First Class (SFC) Christopher Speer had actually survived.

Then years later, "Col. W" changed his own copy of the original memo to also say the combatant who killed Speer had lived. "Col. W" said he changed his report "for the sake of history."

BOTTOM: An Army medic testified via video link from Afghanistan.

43

opening statements     KHADR 8-12-10

OPPOSITE: Prosecutor Jeff Groharing gave an opening statement with a replica of the battlefield as a prop. Behind him, on the monitor, a video of Omar Khadr making a bomb was shown.

LEFT: Delta Force "Sgt. Maj. D." told the court he saw the grenade that killed Army SFC Christopher Speer fly over his head as he entered the compound following the firefight. He said he ran toward the alley where the grenade had originated, saw two people moving, killed one man and shot another person twice in the back. The man he shot was Omar Khadr.

He was pointing to the model of the battlefield as he described exact movements during the battle.

This was right before Omar Khadr's defense attorney Army Lt. Col. Jon Jackson collapsed in court, effectively stalling the trial for two months. Jackson had just recently healed from gall bladder surgery. The fatigue and stress of being Khadr's only trial lawyer was just too physically demanding at the time.

45

## Rather than going to trial, a guilty plea

Oct. 25, 2010: The *second* start of Omar Khadr's trial began two months later. But rather than go through a month of testimony and arguments, Khadr had decided to plead guilty through a pre-trial agreement. The jury did not know the sentencing details of the deal.

Here we see him pleading guilty under oath to charges of spying, conspiracy, providing material support to terrorism, and murder — throwing the grenade that fatally wounded Army SFC Christopher Speer — when he was 15. Under the plea deal he was required to spend at least one more year in Guantanamo before repatriation to Canada. It took nearly two years. He was repatriated to a Canadian prison in September 2012.

From a detailed outline of the charges in a statement released by Army Maj. Tanya Bradsher, a Pentagon spokeswoman: "The Department of Defense announced that Omar Khadr pled guilty today in a military commission. In accordance with a pre-trial agreement, Mr. Khadr admitted, in open court, to committing murder in violation of the law of war, attempted murder in violation of the law of war, providing material support to terrorism, conspiracy, and spying. His sentence will be determined at a hearing that begins Tuesday."

This scene was very quick; I had only as long as it took to read the charges and take an oath — 15 minutes at most. I will admit that sometimes the results are less than desirable, but I have a mantra that often goes through my head while court sketching: "You do what you can do with what time you have." Unlike most courts, where I can polish them afterward, these have to be done before they leave the room — no additions once the court security officer approves a drawing's release. It's sink or swim, and I dogpaddled furiously on this sketch.

Clearance of Sketch Artist Courtroom Drawings

The drawing to which this label is attached has been examined and is cleared for public release.
Signed: _____
Security Officer, Office of Military Commissions

10-26-10 BY Greg Finley NCIS

OPPOSITE: Oct. 25, 2010. Khadr pleaded guilty under oath to all five terrorism charges against him, addressing U.S. Air Force Capt. Michael Grant, left. Presiding: Military Commission Judge Col. Patrick Parrish.

LEFT: Oct. 26, 2010. Second day of trial: We got an audio-visual illustration of what an exploding Russian grenade does to a Humvee and what is used to make a landmine, known as an IED, which Omar Khadr had been seen on video learning to make, shown on the screen behind the witness, on the left. Khadr kept his head in his hands during that testimony and while the video was shown.

48  TOP LEFT: Former NCIS agent Greg Finley testified that he interrogated Omar Khadr around 20 times, and that he never attempted an abusive or coercive interview with Khadr.

BOTTOM LEFT: Edney and Jackson comfort Omar Khadr during a break in trial.

RIGHT: Omar Khadr's Canadian defense lawyer Dennis Edney said he believes Khadr is innocent and had little choice but to make a plea deal in the case.

   "He had to come to a hellish decision ... he had to make it on his own to get out of Guantanamo Bay," Edney told journalists during an informal press meeting after hours.

TOP AND BOTTOM: Forensic psychiatrist Dr. Michael Welner testified that Omar Khadr should not be mainstreamed back into society. Welner testified for hours, so I moved during a break to get different perspectives. Having this kind of flexibility allowed me to get a much broader representation visually.

49

50

TOP LEFT: A Special Forces soldier identified only as "Sgt. Maj. Y" testified on the third day of the sentencing hearing: "For many of us it was the equivalent of losing a brother or sister."

BOTTOM LEFT: Sgt. Layne Morris, a medically retired former Army Special Forces member, who lost sight in one eye during the firefight.

RIGHT: "After nine years, almost a decade of sustained combat, I have lost a lot of friends … and it does not get any easier. But I have not one time seen a loss so absolutely catastrophic," said the soldier identified only as "Captain E."— a close family friend who flew to Afghanistan to replace SFC Speer.

When there's a series of witnesses coming through to testify at a fairly quick pace, I simplify. You can see with my sketch of a soldier testifying anonymously as "Sergeant Major Y" that I started out ambitiously by sketching a bigger scene, then focused on the main subject. He was highly decorated, which I wanted to show, and I got caught up in illustrating that, and showing that he spoke toward the jury: symbolized by those awkward blue tabs. By the time I'd finished filling him in, his testimony had ended. I saw several others waiting in the gallery to testify, so I knew that these next few would be just witness sketches and to build out from there if I had the time. These witness sketches were important, because many of them declined to be photographed.

ance of Sketch Artist Courtroom Drawings

drawing to which this label is applied has been examined and
eared for public release
ed:
rity Officer, Office of Military Commissions

KHADR TO COURT    10/30/10

ABOVE: Oct. 30, 2010. Omar Khadr listens
to the closing arguments of both the
prosecution and defense on the final
day of court before the military panel
went into seclusion to decide a verdict.

LEFT: As is often the case in a courtroom, the briefest of moments can be
poignant and telling. I had sketched
Omar Khadr in just about every way,
except how he entered the court. This
was literally just minutes — a visual
snapshot — but something worth
showing. He was brought in with his
hands out front, bookended by uniden-
tified security that held him lightly but
firmly by the wrists, one hand on top,
one on bottom.

    His guards were surprised and
pleased to see themselves in a sketch,
which they, as well as the court security
officers, got to approve for release. This
sketch got wide usage.

10/20/10

I am mad at you for what you did to my family. Because of you my dad never got to see me play soccer or see me go into kindergarden. You make me really sad and mad at you because of that.

By Taryn Speer

PROSECUTION EXHIBIT
~~FOR IDENTIFICATION~~
PAGE 1 OF 1

There are many rules I follow as a sketch artist in Guantanamo, but one of the most sensitive and mindful ones is how I interact with family members who have lost loved ones and are attending court sessions, known as Victim Family Members (VFM). The Pentagon forbids reporters from talking to these people, official guests at Guantanamo, unless he or she has explicitly agreed to it.

Tabitha Speer, the widow of the medic that Omar Khadr ultimately admitted to killing in a grenade attack, was expected to testify that day. She had been present the whole time and I was told not to draw her. So for several days I kept a very respectful distance. But this day was important: She would testify, and I wanted to know how to handle it. Would I draw her as a ghost-faced figure, or with details? I made my way over when I saw her enter with her military escort and, in her presence, asked the escort if I had permission to sketch her. I always get a queasy ghoulish feeling, because I never want to seem opportunistic and callous, but I also want to get the truest images possible out there. People would *want* to see her.

She looked at me, nodded and said, "Yes, she can draw me." She followed up with a "thank you."

It was dramatic when she got on the stand, with a projection of Chris Speer holding his children on the screen behind her. She said the only promise she has ever failed to keep was the one she made to her daughter — that she would "bring her daddy home." She spoke about her marriage to Speer and who he was as a person.

The only time she spoke directly to Khadr, she called him "someone who is so unworthy" who had "stole[n] all this from" her children, and read a letter the kids wrote to him, shown at right.

There were not many dry eyes in court during her testimony. To me, the whole case came down to: Nature or Nurture? Khadr was a child who was raised by a radical al-Qaida father and was now a young man who had lived behind bars for most of his teens. Does that make what he did right? No. But opinions are not the job of a court artist: the main importance is always to draw exactly what I see people doing, how they sit or gesture, in an honest and neutral way.

KHADR — TABITHA SPEER
(WIDOW)
10/28/10

## Khadr's Statement

*My name is Omar Khadr. I'm 24 years old. I finished 8th grade. My hobbies are sports and reading. I decided to plead guilty to take responsibility for the acts I've done …*

*Firstly, I lost my sight in my left eye. And my right eye was severely wounded. I still experience problems with my right eye. I have a cataract and shrapnel. I've been notified by medical staff that I might lose my vision from my injuries. I was shot twice in my back. Once in my left shoulder, another in my back and they both exited from my chest …*

*That's my biggest dream and biggest wish, to get out of this place. Because, being in this place, I've really known and understood the wonders and beauties of life I haven't experienced before. I would really like to have a chance to experience these things.*

*The first thing is school and knowledge, have the chance to have true relationships, an experience I've never had in my life. And almost everything else in life. Education is knowledge and I have a fascination with knowledge. I just feel it's something beautiful to understand and know and have a sense of everything in life …*

*The most important thing that I wish for is being a doctor of medicine. That's because, me personally, I've experienced from my injuries physical pain and I've experienced like emotional pains. I know what pain means. I'd really love to relieve a person who is suffering from such pain.*

*During my time here, as Nelson Mandela says, in prison, the most thing you have is time to think about things. I've had a lot of time to think about things. I came to a conclusion that hate, first thing is, you're not going to gain anything with hate. Second thing, it's more destructive than constructive. Third thing: I came to a conclusion that love and forgiveness are more constructive and will bring people together and will give them understanding and will solve a lot of problems … [Standing, to Tabitha Speer]: I'm really, really sorry for the pain I've caused you and your family. I wish I could do something that would take this pain away from you. This is all I can say.*

Khadr stood and apologized to Tabitha Speer, who shook her head "no" and wept.

TOP: Oct. 29, 2010. Canadian professor Arlette Zinck testified that she had been corresponding with Omar Khadr, and Edmonton University would offer him assistance to study there upon his release from prison. She had visited Guantanamo to provide Khadr with a United States-approved curriculum, which included Canadian literature, and called him an eager student.

BOTTOM LEFT: Prosecutor Jeffrey Groharing addressed the military panel, seen as blue numbered cards, in closing arguments. Toronto-born detainee Khadr, who pleaded guilty to five war crimes, listened at the far left. Groharing had prosecuted the Khadr case for years, starting as an active-duty Marine and then, after he retired, as a U.S. government civilian lawyer.

BOTTOM RIGHT: I was sitting behind the prosecution, just short of actually being *in* the active court space, and I had an almost unobstructed view of Omar Khadr's face.

OPPOSITE: The verdict finally came late in the day on Sunday, Oct. 31, 2010 – Halloween. The jury handed down a 40-year sentence, sending a strong message. But they didn't know that a prior plea deal dictated that Khadr would serve at most eight more years — at least one more year in Guantanamo, the rest of the time in Canada. He ended up not leaving Gitmo until 2012, when he was returned to Canada.

OCT. 31, 2010   KHADR VERDICT

# ON JANET HAMLIN

by Army Lt. Col. Jon Jackson, Defense Lawyer

I have served my country as a Judge Advocate in the United States Army for more than 16 years. Serving as a defense lawyer in the Office of the Chief Defense Counsel in the Military Commissions has been the most challenging assignment of my career. Military commission defense lawyers, whether military or civilian, are fighting to ensure that our country adheres to the Rule of Law regardless of who is accused of a crime.

Whether a person supports the military commission process or not, everyone agrees that these cases are of incredible importance. Because photography and recorded video is prohibited during trial, Janet Hamlin serves as the visual historian for the Military Commissions. Her courtroom sketches demonstrate an incredible ability to tell the story of a case because of their accuracy and attention to detail.

Hamlin effectively and efficiently accomplishes the task of sketching a brief moment of time in the courtroom, despite being in one of the most bizarre environments on Earth. Many reading this will not have been to Guantanamo Bay. Therefore, it is almost impossible to explain how crazy it really is. But if you imagine working at a place where the rules and people change every day, you might begin to understand.

Finally, Hamlin believes in the integrity of her work. Therefore, when you see her work, you can trust its accuracy. On one occasion a particularly difficult lawyer wanted changes made to one of her sketches. I overheard the conversation, and Hamlin refused to make the changes (and she was right!). She handled that lawyer as I am sure she handles most difficult situations in her life: with a pleasant demeanor and a calm, even temperament. I am proud to know her and call her a friend. ★

OCT 29, 2010

JACKSON READING OMAR'S STATEMENT

# SALIM HAMDAN
## Osama bin Laden's Driver

July 23, 2008. Whisked into the courtroom ahead of the media, I was asked to get a sketch of Hamdan out as soon as possible. This was a huge story. Just as I began sketching, I was told to leave the court and sit in the hallway until the current witness had finished; he was a secret agent who did not want to be sketched. I pointed out that nothing I sketch is released without military approval so barring me from the court was unnecessary. But the judge was firm. I was told to go sit in the hallway until called. I managed to finish the drawing by getting glances as the court doors opened and closed and craning my neck to look at a security monitor that was pointed at Hamdan. Once I was allowed back in court, I added the jury and image on the monitor — a diagram showing Hamdan's connection to Osama bin Laden. I had just enough time to get the sketch approved and handed off to the media at first break.

# What Hamdan Was Thinking

Translated by Charles Schmitz,
Hamdan's translator during the trial.

كان اول حضور لى الى المحكمه واول مره ادخل الى
محكمه ومرافعات وقاضى ومحامين من الطرفين  مثل ما
اشوف فى الافلام  واجراءت  وعدم فهمى لاى شى من
القانون واجراءت المحكامات        وهل سوف تكون المحكمه
عادله او على  ما تشتى الحكومه الامريكيه  وعدم
استخدام اى من القانون المدنى او القانون العسكرى
وانشاء قانون  جديد لا يتوفر  فيه اشياء لصالح المعتقل

Salim Hamdan, in response to the sketch at left: *This was the first time I was in court, and the first time I saw the motions and the judge and lawyers from each side like I had seen in the movies, and I didn't understand anything about the law and the court procedures. I wondered whether the trial would be fair, or only what the American government wanted. They weren't using civilian law or military law, and they made up a new law that doesn't offer anything in favor of the prisoner.*

Charles Schmitz (Translator): This drawing depicts a session early in the trial when the government was presenting its case. Since this was the first trial at Guantanamo, we had no idea what to expect. Many of the normal rules of evidence and procedure in U.S. military and civilian law were not being used in Guantanamo, so we were very skeptical about the possibility of Hamdan getting a fair trial.

صحيح كنت اسال المحامي كيف الضباط هم من سيحددو
مصيري وهم من طرف الحكومه حيث انهم لا يعرفون او لا
يفهمون الطباع العربيه او حتى التقاليد اليمنيه على
الاقل وليس لديهم اى فكره عن الاسلام

Salim Hamdan: *I would ask the lawyers how an officer from the side of the government could determine my fate, when they don't know or understand about Arabs or even Yemeni tradition at least, and they have no idea about Islam.*

Charles Schmitz (Translator): This was a difficult day for Hamdan, because the government showed a video of one of his first interrogations in Afghanistan. Reliving that experience was traumatic enough, but Hamdan was also upset because he felt it didn't portray him in a positive light. I had to explain to him that in a jury trial each side has a chance to paint a picture of the truth and of course the government was going to paint a bad picture. We would have a chance to paint our picture of the truth later.

Charles Schmitz (Translator): One of the things that we were very concerned about was the jury. The jury was all U.S. military officers, and we were skeptical that military officers could fairly judge someone who was demonized as not just their enemy, but evil itself: in the end, these particular officers were not swayed by scare tactics and propaganda.

July 24, 2008. The second day of Hamdan's trial. A secret
agent testifies.

Charles Schmitz (Translator): In the Arab world they do not
have jury trials, their trials are by judge, like in continental
Europe, so a lot of my work with Hamdan was explaining
what was going on. Most of the prisoners in Guantanamo
were calling for a boycott of the trials, and Hamdan was also
very skeptical that any justice would be served by the trials.
So I worked hard to make sure that Hamdan understood
what was happening in the trial. Even so, Hamdan had days
when he felt it was useless and he wanted to leave.

اول ما رايت المحلفين وعددهم الكثير مباشرا سالت
المحامى والمترجم ما يشتو هؤلا كلهم وليش موجودين لان
عندنا لايوجد تلك الاجراءت وان عندنا قاضى واحد يكون
فى المحكمه    نعم كثير من المعتقلين طلبو منى عدم
الذهاب الى المحكمه وانه لا توجد اى فائده من المحكمه
لعدم وجود قانون يحكم المحكمه من اجل ان تكون محكمه
عادله    وقد حاول المحامين كثيرا فى اقناعى للحضور
الى المحكمه بعد ان رفضت الحضور الى المحكمه عدة
مرات لعدم وجود اى فائده من المحاكمه

Salim Hamdan: *The first time I saw the jurors, there were so many of*
*them, and I asked the lawyers what all of them wanted and why were*
*they there, because we don't have all of these procedures and there is*
*only a judge. Many of the prisoners asked me not to go to the trial,*
*because there was no benefit in a trial: because there was no law to*
*guarantee a fair trial. The lawyers tried hard to convince me to attend*
*the trial after I refused to attend the trial several times, thinking that*
*there was no benefit in a trial.*

An agent testified while a list of names was projected. This was my final sketch in the Hamdan trial. The media pool had only agreed to a sketch artist for the first two days, so I missed sketching the remainder of the trial and the sentencing.

The prosecution asked for 30 years but the panel gave him 66 months, with credit for time served. Hamdan was the first detainee convicted at trial by a military commission, and first man to be acquitted of a war crime. The panel found him guilty of providing material support for terrorism, but cleared him of a conspiracy charge. In October 2012, an appeals court overturned his conviction.

He is now free and living quietly in Yemen with his family.

Charles Schmitz (Translator): Some of the days of the trial were very long. We listened to simultaneous translation in the headphones, and sometimes the technical legal aspects of the trial were very dry. We would sometimes just talk about other things in the room, like why had someone decided to wear that tie on that particular day, or what was the significance of someone's particular uniform.

لدرجه اننى طلبت من المحامى ما اشنى الحضور الى قاعه المحكمه من الكلام الطويل      وايضا من مشكله انقطاع الصوت فى الترجمه او الترجمه تكوت غير صحيحه فعندما ارجع الى غرفه الانتظار نتكلم عن مشكله انقطاع الصوت او الكلام الطويل والغير مفهوم وانا جالس فى قاعه المحمكه

Salim Hamdan: *I asked the lawyer if I could not be in the courtroom, because there was so much talking and sometimes the sound cut off in the translation, and sometimes the translation was not correct. When we would go to the break room, we would talk about the problems in the translation, the long sessions, and things not being understood while I was in the courtroom.*

Hamlin    7/23/08

## Courtroom 2:
## The Expeditionary Legal Complex

Courtroom 2 was built specifically for the 9/11 trial. A high security — but portable — court, it is surrounded by mesh-enclosed chain-link fences topped with barbed wire. Photography of the outside of the court is strictly forbidden, but the military has given out pictures of the inside for media purposes.

Behind the court there is a holding cell for detainees as well as SCIFs (which stands for Sensitive Compartmented Information Facility — the C is pronounced like a K), and as various structures for security.

*Security* is the key word here. An escort walks us from McCalla Hangar to a security checkpoint just outside the fenced-in court. There we go through metal detectors and have our things scanned and searched. If the metal detector is set off, a soldier, holding a sensitive metal-detecting wand, body-scans us individually (it's like what one goes through to fly these days). My drawing kit is also opened and inspected. I pre-sharpen all my pencils, because absolutely no blades are allowed in court.

For a long while, reporters were forbidden from bringing their own pens, or pads that had spiral wires holding them together. A guard at the court would issue each reporter a pen.

There is one less metal detecting station/checkpoint now, but it used to be that the process would be repeated: metal detector, drawing-kit inspection. It's about 25 feet along a fence-lined path to a booth and entry to the actual court compound.

Our media badges are checked and logged in. We also have to carry our passports, which we sometimes have to show.

We move toward the court. Our escort keys in the code to unlock the door and we enter, get logged in by our badge number, and are told our assigned seats. We can leave the court to use the restrooms, etc., but cannot leave the fenced-in compound unescorted. Even though court is within easy walking distance, we leave about an hour early to pass through and get seated.

Family members go through this too, entering and exiting ahead of us to keep us separate.

We all sit in back of the court behind soundproof glass windows, in the viewing area. Sound is delayed by 40 seconds, so the security officer can apply white noise if something is said that we are not allowed to hear.

What we are seeing looks like a badly dubbed movie as a result.

The windows are each three panes thick and soundproof, with a little reflective kickback — not easy to draw through. Because there are so many people between my view and the subjects, I sometimes stand to get a better view. Plastic, magnifying spectator glasses help with far-away details.

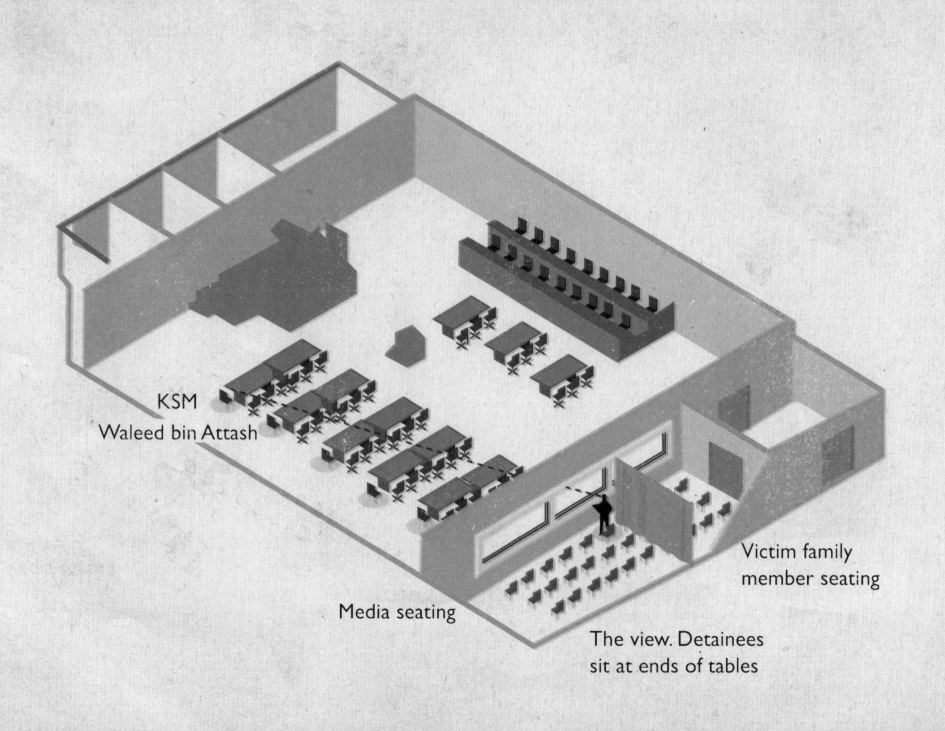

KSM
Waleed bin Attash

Media seating

Victim family
member seating

The view. Detainees
sit at ends of tables

# ALI HAMZA AL BAHLUL

A military jury convicted Ali Hamza al Bahlul, the second war crimes conviction. He was found guilty because he created an al-Qaida recruiting video as Osama bin Laden's media secretary. Sentencing would be read later that day. I drew these images in June, when I had been sent to draw the 9/11 co-conspirators. A new courtroom had been constructed especially for the high security cases, and I wanted to sketch as much as I could to get a feel for the environment, which is a room at the back of the court for media, behind thick glass windows. It was the first time the court was being used in its official capacity, so there were a few delays during audio cutout. At one point the judge left his post just to keep the tribunal moving forward.

69

OPPOSITE: My first practice run in Courtroom 2 yielded the only image of accused al-Qaida propagandist Ali Hamza al Bahlul. During the hearing Bahlul waved a boycott sign (inset).

LEFT: Kinks were still being worked out in Courtroom 2. The judge's microphone kept malfunctioning, so the judge moved to the defense's table to go through the proceedings without further delay.

# AL QOSI
## Al-Qaida Cook

Ibrahim Ahmed Mahmoud al Qosi was one of the first detainees brought to Guantanamo in January 2002, when the Bush administration opened the prison, and the first person sentenced in Courtroom 2 that I sketched. It was a busy time, because Omar Khadr was in court at the same time in Courtroom 1.

I dashed from one court to the other over the course of a few days: a little tricky with all the security, but the military made a point of helping me get between them as quickly as possible.

On July 7, 2010, al Qosi pleaded guilty to conspiracy and supporting terrorism, and confessed that he had followed Osama bin Laden to Afghanistan in 1996 where he performed menial tasks, including running a kitchen and sometimes driving for bin Laden's camp compound. He claimed to have had no knowledge of the 9/11 terrorist attacks.

I was there to sketch the sentencing; the commission gave him 14 years in prison on top of the eight years he had been held at Guantanamo at that point. Under the plea deal, 12 years of the prison sentence were suspended. So he was sent home to Sudan on July 11, 2012, becoming the first detainee convicted during the Obama administration sent back to his country.

Al-Qaida cook from Sudan, Ibrahim al Qosi, attended his war crimes trial at the Camp Justice compound on Guantanamo Bay.

al Qosi 8/11/10

TOP: Ibrahim al Qosi listens to arguments. On the right, the military jury listens. It's the first time I sketched a jury in Courtroom 2, and probably the last (see explanation below). Presiding as judge is Lt. Col. Nancy Paul.

MIDDLE: Al Qosi's defense attorney at the time, Navy Cmdr. Suzanne Lachelier, addressed the military panel, shown symbolically as blue tabs. I had been instructed I could not draw them in the Omar Khadr hearings, which were going on at the same time in Court-room 1. To be on the safe side, I used the same symbolic blue tabs in Courtroom 2 as well.

BOTTOM: Wednesday, Aug. 11, 2010. Defense attorney Paul Reichler gave the closing arguments to the panel in con-sideration of detainee Ibrahim al Qosi for sentencing in his war crimes trial.

June 6, 2008. Pictured top to bottom: Marine Col. Ralph H. Kohlman, presiding: Khalid Sheikh Mohammed, Walid bin Attash, Ramzi bin al Shibh, Ammar al Baluchi, and Mustafa al Hawsawi for the first time in Guantanamo court. When the judge spoke to Mohammed, he responded by standing up, chanting, and welcoming martyrdom. I had to quickly redraw and reposition him standing.

approved

6-6-2008

# KHALID SHEIKH MOHAMMED AND "THE NOSE"

When I got the call from CNN to sketch the arraignment of the accused 9/11 mastermind I knew it was going to be a big story and a lot of pressure, but I never expected to become part of the controversy.

It all started fairly benignly. I was asked to sketch a detailed view of Mohammed, who was known by his initials, KSM. If there was enough time, I was instructed to follow up with a group sketch — all to be released to the news media by the first morning recess.

I figured there would be a few hours at least, since there were five accused. But you never know. It could be one hour or 13, as we would find out in a future arraignment.

So I went in tightly coiled, but ready. I knew Courtroom 2 was going to be challenging, sketching from the back and behind soundproof windows in the spectators' gallery. My heart sank the moment I stepped inside and looked. Every table in the court was filled; KSM and the other accused were at the far end of each defense table, tiny heads seemingly far, far away. When I sat down, I could see even less. So I decided to stand with my pastels piled on the drawing board — there was no table, and no time to get one — and do my best.

KSM seemed to be posing for me, turning my way and chatting with Walid bin Attash, who sat right behind him. As I laid his features out, I could tell it was a little off. Standing, moving my supplies around, I was tense and stiff. The likeness was off, his nose too long —

but I needed to get that group drawing in and had to move on. I put it on the floor and started the group sketch. At the first break, the court security officer came to the spectator's gallery to review my sketches. The rest would become history, best described in the excerpt from *The New Yorker* on the following page. In short, KSM did not like how his nose was drawn, and I had to leave the sketch there, go back to the media, get a printout, and head back to fix the drawing before it could go out. Right away the media knew there was a story — how can KSM have the right to reject a sketch and make the artist redo it? Especially after claiming responsibility for 9/11 and wanting to be martyred! But he did have that right, and it went on to become a story in and of itself: profiled in a "Talk of the Town" article in *The New Yorker*, the law blog of *Wall Street Journal*, NPR, BBC, parodied by Jon Stewart and Stephen Colbert, *Time* magazine's "quote of the week" — there was sudden worldwide interest in what I, the artist, had to say about this.

## Excerpt from *The New Yorker*'s "Talk of the Town" published July 7, 2008, by Ben McGrath

Guantánamo visit No. 5 took place in early June, when the prison's most infamous inmate, the alleged terrorist mastermind Khalid Sheikh Mohammed —called K.S.M. for short—was due in court. After a harrowing flight aboard a C-130 Hercules ("It looks like something you would see in an old John Wayne movie—it's like a flying garage"), Hamlin was escorted to a viewing room, separated from the court by glass. No binoculars or other visual aids were allowed, and audio was piped in on a twenty-second delay. "So it was like watching a bad Japanese movie," she said. "Imagine yourself in a room behind the court, and K.S.M. was probably a few trees back," she continued, looking out the window toward her back yard, where her dog, Molly, was yelping to be let in. "He had these big goggles on, with an elastic safety strap, and he would do this occasionally"— she craned her neck and raised her hand to an imaginary set of goggles—"and then look at me, as if posing." Hamlin was surprised at K.S.M.'s vanity, given his famously unkempt appearance upon his apprehension, in 2003, but in captivity he had acquired a dignified look: much leaner, and with a Merlinesque gray beard. Hamlin did her best to sketch a decent likeness, but the goggles and the beard may have blinded her to the subtleties of his facial features. She gave him "quite the beak," she admitted.

K.S.M. was not pleased. During a break in the proceedings, Hamlin saw Mohammed gesturing in disapproval as he examined her work. "They said, 'Um, listen, K.S.M. doesn't want to O.K. this,'" she recalled. "He says, 'The nose is wrong, and tell the artist to go get my F.B.I. picture off the Internet and use that as a reference to fix it.'" So began an hour-long process in which Hamlin was escorted to the media tent, where she printed out an image before returning—"always the gate, the search, the wand"—to make reparations. The picture was almost certainly not the F.B.I. photograph that K.S.M. had in mind. "It's that one where he's in a T-shirt, looking really disheveled," she said. Still, Mohammed had a point. Whatever the other indignities of the photo, which made him look like an especially hirsute DWI offender, it showed a relatively short and slender nose compared with the proboscis that Hamlin had given him. She softened the edges before resubmitting it.

LEFT: June 5, 2008. The infamous "Nose" sketch: The original, offending nose is buried under layers of pastel on this reworked sketch.

# 9/11 Co-Conspirators

TOP: Ammar al Baluchi. In order to get these views, I sketched from glances at the monitors that show the courtroom from specially mounted security cameras. It was the only way I could see their faces to sketch; they sat at table ends, turned slightly, facing the judge inside the court.

MIDDLE: Ramzi bin al Shibh (center right), a suspect in the Sept. 11 attacks co-conspirator case, sits with one of his defense lawyers, Tom Durkin.

BOTTOM: Thursday, June 5, 2008. Mustafa al Hawsawi, a suspect in the Sept. 11 attacks co-conspirator case.

OPPOSITE: Dec. 8, 2008. The 9/11 co-conspirators made a second appearance in court for a hearing. For the first time ever, 9/11 victim family members were flown in to watch the hearing. For privacy reasons, they sat behind a blue curtain. The ones that allowed me to sketch them sat out front, holding photo books of their loved ones. It was heartbreaking.

The 9/11 arraignment included the following five men being charged together:

KHALID SHEIKH MOHAMMED who, after he got to Guantanamo in 2006, after 183 rounds of waterboarding, said he planned the 9/11 attacks "from A to Z," and also claimed responsibility for killing *Wall Street Journal* reporter Daniel Pearl, plus numerous other terrorism plots.

WALID BIN ATTASH, accused of running an al-Qaida training camp in Afghanistan, where some of the 19 September 11 hijackers were trained.

RAMZI BIN AL SHIBH, accused of organizing the German cell of hijackers and helping move their finances to the United States, where they attended flight schools.

AMMAR AL BALUCHI, accused of helping some of the hijackers get money and travel to the United States. He's Mohammed's nephew.

MUSTAFA AL HAWSAWI, accused of helping some of the hijackers get typical American clothing, traveler's checks, and credit cards.

RIGHT: Dec. 8, 2008. Khalid Sheikh Mohammed, Walid bin Attash, Ramzi bin al Shibh, Ammar al Baluchi, and Mustafa al Hawsawi, Sept. 11, 2001 attack co-defendants, sit during a hearing at the Guantanamo war crimes court. To the right, behind glass in the viewing booth in the back of the court, the 9/11 victim family members observe. I had not yet solved the visual problem of including them and what they were looking at all in one scene without it looking awkward: though on the right, it is starting to come together. As the day came to a close, one of the defendants folded a paper airplane and tossed it in the direction of the family members.

OPPOSITE: Jan. 19, 2009. KSM kept stroking his beard, pulling it into two devilish points. At the bottom, closest to us, sat Mustafa al Hawsawi, who seemed to want to disappear under his head covering. He sat in a hunched-over, hidden position, not really interacting with the others much.

78

12/8/2008

## Obama Takes Office

Jan. 20, 2009. President Obama was being inaugurated, as seen on TV broadcasts at a Guantanamo Bay dining hall facility. I went with some of the reporters to cover some troops' reactions to the inauguration.

That night, at around 11 p.M., word reached us that Obama was putting the Guantanamo hearings on hold. I have a memory of Reuters correspondent Jane Sutton sprinting to the media center in her pajamas to write the breaking news, leading the pack. They worked well into the night, and we thought this would very likely be our last trip.

Clearance of Sketch Artist Courtroom Drawings

The drawing to which this label is attached has
been examined and is cleared for public release
Signed: James R. Farrell 20 Jan 09
Security Officer, Office of Military Commissions

9/11 commissions

1/21/09

Jan. 21, 2009. The day after Obama's
inauguration, 9/11 co-conspirators
learned of his plan to suspend the
Guantanamo hearings. Each detainee
had a manila folder placed where he
sat, which informed him of the Obama
administration suspension.

RIGHT: July 16, 2009. Family members of victims of the Sept. 11, 2001 attacks observed courtroom proceedings during hearings for the five alleged Sept. 11 conspirators, inside the courthouse at the Camp Justice compound for the U.S. war crimes trial. Once arraigned, the detainees were given the choice to not attend, which Khalid Sheikh Mohammed and four fellow Sept. 11, 2001 attack defendants accepted. Family members who flew all the way to Cuba came to a court with five empty defendant seats. Below one, you can see shackles for one of the detainees who was on psychotropic medication; they wanted the additional security option. My challenge was to make a sketch that told a story for news media, even without the defendants. To me, it was a powerful image to show the empty seats in an otherwise full courtroom from the family members' point of view. By skewing perspective, I was able to do that.

OPPOSITE: July 17, 2009. KSM and Walid bin Attash chose to boycott the hearing on this day. To the judge's left you can see the security officer and his red light. He is the one that can press a mute button that replaces courtroom audio feeds to the public with white noise if he suspects that something being said is classified. He is also the person who goes over my drawings and signs off on them before they can be released.

Clearance of Sketch Artist Courtroom Drawings

The drawing to which this label is attached has
been examined and is cleared for public release
Signed: _____
Security Officer, Office of Military Commissions

7/16/09    9/11 CO-CONSPIRATORS

# A MULTIMEDIA JOURNALIST'S VIEWPOINT

by Muna Shikaki, Al-Arabiya

Hamlin's sketches are like small dioramas or Persian miniature paintings. One look and you understand the context of what's going on in court. But then the real pleasure comes from carefully observing all the details and multiple side stories that each of the characters in the sketch tell. As a videographer, this means just one of Hamlin's drawings allows me to zoom in so the audience sees the interaction between the judge and the lawyer in one corner. In another corner we see the detainee's expressions, and sometimes her sketches are the only way to see how a detainee has aged: whether he's grown a beard, what clothing he decided to wear, whether he paid attention in court. Yet another corner will show victims' family members in court. All of this from one sketch.

Being a videographer in Guantanamo can be very frustrating. Everyone wants to see what the base is like, where the prisoners are held, what the "expeditionary" courts are made of. Yet military censorship rules, vague in some cases and strictly detailed in others, make it impossible to convey any of this: no panoramas, no overview shots, not that antenna, but oh yes, this one's okay, no detainee faces, no wait, no detainee "defining features" either (like prosthetic legs). Can we make out that sailor's eyes? Oh, then delete him. Every young censor-sailor exercises his or her own interpretation of the rules. Hamlin's sketches are a wonderful antidote to that as she churns out one beautifully detailed scene after the other. She is the only reason I am able to cover these events as a broadcast journalist who relies on visuals to tell a story. ★

*Al-Arabiya's Muna Shikaki at work, carefully videotaping imagery, which will be combed over and edited. No faces or identifying details of detainees can be captured.*

# 9/11 TRIAL:
# SECOND TIME AROUND

The highly anticipated return of the alleged mastermind had occurred — no one could predict how he would react — and this was the first time he was seen in public after a several-year hiatus and withdrawal of his first charges.

This time, he wore lightweight glasses and his beard was dyed henna red. He took his seat and began reading, refusing to respond to the judge. The others followed suit. All refused to wear headsets broadcasting the Arabic translations; their lawyers said the ear coverings reminded them of their torture. So translators were lined up, microphones given, and they translated out loud, word for word.

An arraignment would typically last one to three hours. This one stretched across 13. In part, this was because of simultaneous translation. But prayer breaks, and one defendant's insistence that the entire charge sheet be read aloud, prolonged it even more.

BOTTOM: Army Col. James L. Pohl, the Chief of the Military Commissions judiciary, assigned himself to this case, and also to preside at the trial of the alleged U.S.S. Cole bomber, Abd al Rahim al Nashiri. Both are death penalty cases.

He is the most senior judge in the U.S. Army, and currently the only judge actively hearing cases at Camp Justice.

85

In order to sketch the faces of the detainees from the front, I have to draw from monitors that show images from court-run security cameras. The military wouldn't let me inside the court, but did let me go to a separate building where I could watch the proceedings on two split-screen monitors showing static views of key individuals face-forward. The monitor is a little fuzzy, and sometimes the colors are not quite true. KSM's beard, for example, looked brown, when in fact it was cherry-red. But these monitors have given me the chance to capture so much more of what is going on in the court from different vantage points.

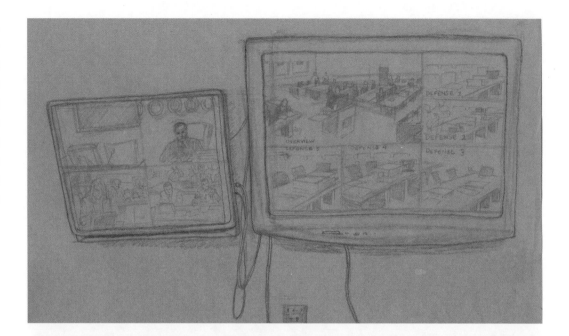

BOTTOM RIGHT: May 5, 2012. Walid bin Attash had grown out his hair, and he was initially brought into the courtroom strapped to a chair: by one account, because he was refusing to attend. Attendance at the arraignment is mandatory. The accused can voluntarily opt out of other hearings. But on this day, bin Attash was brought in, and his prosthetic leg was carried in separately.

TOP LEFT: Ammar al Baluchi read the Quran during his arraignment.

TOP RIGHT: Ramzi bin al Shibh read the Quran during his arraignment.

BOTTOM LEFT: Mustafa al Hawsawi read the Quran during his arraignment.

BOTTOM RIGHT: During a break in the arraignment, lawyer David Nevin was pointing something out to his client, KSM. Although none of the accused would answer the judge, and sat through the proceedings in stony silence, they were quite animated during recesses — talking among themselves and with their attorneys.

87

The detainees were allowed 45-minute breaks to pray in court during the arraignment. They got up, unfurled their prayer rugs and, with KSM leading, bowed their heads to the floor in traditional prayer, while soldiers stood guard along the walls and others milled around the court. After they finished praying, they chatted among themselves until court reconvened. They had several prayer breaks; the arraignment lasted over 13 hours.

Detainees 5-5-12
praying before noon session

Family members watched the arraignment from the viewing gallery. I can only sketch them with permission. Sometimes I get requests to include them in a sketch, so I make a point of doing so whenever possible. Family members from top to bottom: Eddie Bracken; a woman who wished to remain anonymous; Mary Henwood-Klotz; and Tara Henwood-Butzbaugh.

5-5-12

TOP: Cheryl Bormann, defense attorney for Walid bin Attash, wore a hijab and asked the other women in the courtroom to also dress modestly. When I saw her argue in that attire, I dashed this sketch out, because it was such a strong visual.

BOTTOM: During breaks in the arraignment, KSM and others were free to talk to each other. Here, KSM talks to Walid bin Attash.

KSM DURING LUNCH BREAK - HOLDING UP DOCUMENT

## 9/11 TRIAL:
## THE FIRST HEARING

October 2012. At one point during a break, KSM held up a photograph of what appeared to be a structure in the desert. He gestured to it while addressing his attorney, David Nevin. I quickly sketched this, because rarely do I get a live view of KSM's face in court. His beard was an even more startling red, no longer henna-like. We found out later that he used berry juice and other things from his meals to create the dye for it. The photo he was holding was interesting to me. Anything visual and different is important to capture.

91

92

TOP LEFT: KSM with his legal defense team: He was very involved the whole time. From left to right: civilian lead defense attorney David Nevin, Army Cpt. Jason D. Wright, Marine Corps Maj. Derek Poteet, and KSM.

TOP RIGHT: Yemeni Ramzi bin al Shibh, one of the five accused, chose his own clothing during the hearings in October 2012.

BOTTOM LEFT: Mustafa al Hawsawi, one of the five accused, sat with his translator during the hearings in October 2012.

BOTTOM RIGHT: Ramzi bin al Shibh with his legal defense team. On left: James G. Connell III.

In the front, viewing, is victim family member Merrilly Noeth. Only two of the five detainees showed up for this morning session: front, Walid bin Attash and Ramzi bin al Shibh.

93

I just had to capture this scene of
Cheryl Bormann addressing the judge
in her hijab.

94

Oct. 17, 2012. Khalid Sheikh Mohammed wore a camouflage vest to
court. Army Col. James L. Pohl, the
judge, is shown in back with a court
security officer at his left. Both Pohl
and the security officer have buttons to
mute, with white noise, testimony they
suspect may be classified; the security
officer also reviews my sketches
before releasing them.

Today's camouflage-vest garb
caused a stir. KSM has argued that he
is a warrior, and his lawyers got the
judge to agree to let him wear para-
military clothing to court. The vest is a
hunting vest and can be found at Sears.

95

10/17/12    KSM WEARING CAMOFLAGE VEST    9/11 PRETRIAL HEARINGS

ALEXANDRA SCOTT        MARTIN TOYEN        DORINE TOYEN

10-18-12

CONNELL
ADDRESSES
JUDGE POHL
ON PROTECTIVE
ORDERS

PRIOR RESTRAINT

OPPOSITE: Alexandra Scott (left), who lost her father Randy Scott, 48, of Stanford, Conn., sits beside Martin and Dorine Toyen (right), who lost their daughter Amy, 24, of Avon, Conn., on the fourth day of pre-trial hearings in the 9/11 war crimes prosecution.

TOP LEFT: Oct. 17, 2012. On the third day of 9/11 pre-trial hearings, KSM spoke with Marine Maj. Derek Poteet. KSM's nephew Ammar al Baluchi sat in back with his translator.

BOTTOM LEFT: KSM addressed Judge James L. Pohl, an Army colonel, during the third day of 9/11 pre-trial hearings.
   Far left: Army Cpt. Jason Wright and Marine Maj. Derek Poteet. His lawyers covered their heads and busied themselves while KSM spoke for about 15 minutes.
   An Excerpt: "Your blood is not made of gold and ours is made out of water. We are all human beings. Thank you."

RIGHT: Judge Pohl responded that was the "last time" KSM would be allowed to speak his opinions in court.

9/11 PRET
10-18-12    HEARING
PROSECU

OPPOSITE: Here's a scene of the prosecution team in court on the fourth day of pre-trial hearings in the 9/11 war crimes case.

LEFT: Victim family members listen to American Civil Liberties Union (ACLU) lawyer Hina Shamsi address the court. From left to right: victim family members Gordon Haberman, Kathy Haberman, Jo Acquaviva, and Alfred Acquaviva.

The previous day, Shamsi had argued that a court-approved 40-second sound delay to the public was unconstitutional censorship. "You know, it should go without saying, but perhaps the CIA needs to hear it: Thoughts, experiences, and memories belong to human beings," she said. "They do not belong to the government." The judge, Army Col. James Pohl, ultimately rejected her motion.

RIGHT: A U.S. military officer testified that the detainees all chose to exercise their option of not attending the proceedings that day.

OPPOSITE LEFT: James G. Connell III, defense lawyer for Ammar al Baluchi.

OPPOSITE RIGHT: Oct. 18, 2012. Defense lawyer Cheryl Bormann spoke with Judge Pohl as the first hearing wound down. Since no detainees were present, she did not wear her hijab.

HEARINGS

10-18-12

Cheryl BORMANN      9/11 Pretrial
JUDGE POHL           HEARINGS

102

LEFT: Prosecutor Clay Trivett

CENTER: Navy Cmdr. Walter Ruiz

RIGHT: Army Maj. Rob McGovern, a
retired NFL player. Deeply affected
by the 9/11 attacks, he spent four
days helping recover remains from
the World Trade Center (WTC)
rubble. Eleven years later, McGovern
joined the prosecution team in the
case against the five accused 9/11
conspirators.

Clearance of Sketch Artist Courtroom Drawing
The Drawing to Which this Label is Attached Has
Been Examined and is Cleared for Public Release.
Signed: M.A.A.

# 9/11 TRIAL PREPARATION 2013, PRE-TRIAL HEARINGS BEGIN

9/11 hearings were underway, with three of the accused wearing camouflage. From left to right sit Ramzi, Walid bin Attash, and Khalid Sheikh Mohammed. Judge Pohl presides, a security officer sits behind the monitor, and defense attorney Cheryl Bormann wears a hijab at the podium.

We met the victim family members on the first day we arrived this trip, with an excellent exchange during a meet-and-greet. As a result of this, I think, for the first time ever, the *entire* group of victim family members wanted to be in a sketch.

I had to think about how to get them all in one sketch, and then it came to me: draw them watching the hearings, from their point of view. They had traveled far to witness this, and had suffered the loss of their loved ones. There was some comfort for them to watch these hearings.

LEFT: Families of 9/11 victims brought to Guantanamo to observe the 9/11 hearings. Back row: Military Commissions escorts Patricia Moss and Domini McDonald. Second row, back to front: Debra Strickland, Phyllis Rodriguez, Joyce Woods, and John Woods. Front row, back to front: Loreen Sellitto, Matt Sellitto, Anne Gabriel, and Christopher Gabriel.

106

9/11 HEARING   JAN 28, 2013
KSM'S DEFENSE  NEVIN AT PODIUM

DEFENSE
WALTER RUIZ ADDRESSING JUDGE POHL
RE$ ACCESS TO DETAINEES

1-29-13 MORNING SESSION

OPPOSITE: A view of all five accused, with a security guard behind the monitor. KSM's defending attorney, David Nevin, addresses the judge.

RIGHT: At the podium, defense attorney Walter Ruiz argues for better access to clients; he requests defense be allowed to spend 48 hours in the Camp 7 compound to assess their living conditions.

McGOVERN AT PODIUM

OPPOSITE: Jan. 29, 2013. In this Pentagon-approved sketch, 9/11 hearings continue a second day. At the podium, case prosecutor Army Maj. Robert McGovern addresses the judge. McGovern had been a pro football player. During 9/11, he was a volunteer responder.

LEFT: Army Maj. Michael Griffin testified on the second day of the 9/11 hearings that he verified that none of the five accused chose to attend.

RIGHT: Jan. 29, 2013. 9/11 hearings continue a second day; civilian lawyer James Connell defends Ammar al Baluchi.

OPPOSITE: Jan. 31, 2013. A different perspective from the viewing gallery shows several monitors for close-up views of whoever is speaking at the time.

110

Clearance of Sketch Artist Courtroom Drawing
The Drawing to Which this Label is Attached Has
Been Examined and is Cleared for Public Release.
Signed:
Court Security Officer
Office of Military Commission

JAN. 31, 2013                    9/11 HEARINGS

GEN. MARTINS ADDRESSING JUDGE POHL

# Chief Prosecutor Mark Martins' Remarks At Guantanamo Bay: 31 January 2013

Good afternoon. This week the military commission convened to try the charges against Khalid Shaikh Mohammad, Walid Muhammad Salih Mubarak Bin 'Attash, Ramzi bin al Shibh, Ammar al Baluchi, and Mustafa al Hawsawi [and] considered pre-trial issues raised by the defense and the prosecution. The Judge examined the parties' written briefs and heard oral argument. These pre-trial sessions are an indispensable part of this sharply adversarial process and are necessary to the fair and open administration of justice.

This week, the Judge ruled on six (6) motions, raising the total number of rulings to twenty five (25). The defense withdrew one (1) motion, and two (2) others were dismissed as moot. Other motions argued, once ruled upon, will settle the outstanding issues regarding Protective Order #1 and thus will enable the defense to analyze a great amount of classified information while also protecting that information.

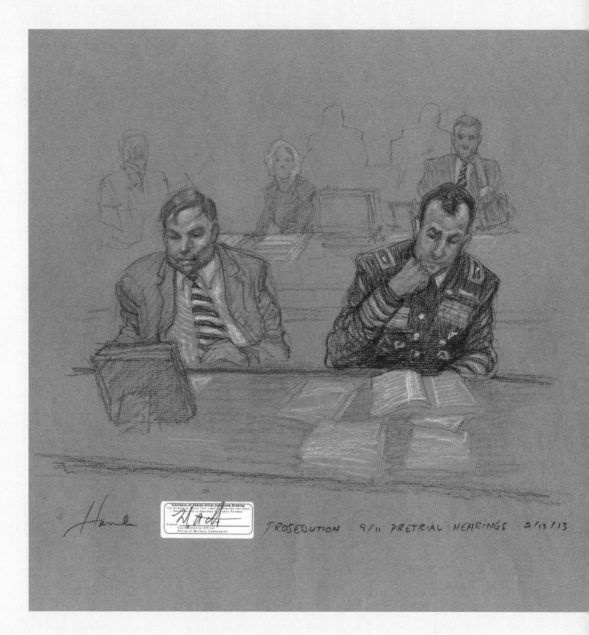

RIGHT: Feb. 12, 2013. Prosecutors Robert Swann (at left) and Army Brig. Gen. Mark Martins.

# Chief Prosecutor Mark Martins' Remarks At Guantanamo Bay: 10 February 2013

Tomorrow is the first of four scheduled days of pre-trial sessions in the case of United States versus Khalid Shaikh Mohammad and four co-accused who stand charged with plotting the attacks of September 11, 2001. The charges allege that the accused and their fellow plotters—including Usama Bin Laden, as well as four individuals who had received pilot training and fifteen so-called muscle hijackers:

forged identify and travel documents and
    fraudulently opened bank accounts;
found sanctuary in ungoverned regions and
    forbidding terrain;
trained participants in camps and safe-houses;
coordinated operations and recruited participants
    via the internet and email;
leveraged off-the-shelf technologies such as global
    positioning system receivers;
hid among civilian travelers and secreted weapons
    in carry-on bags;
practiced operational security while studying
    security lapses by authorities;
rehearsed their attacks and precursor actions to
    eliminate shortcomings.

Such preparations culminated in the hijacking and crashing of civilian airliners into buildings in New York, Washington, D.C., and a field in Pennsylvania, killing nearly 3,000 persons. I emphasize that the charges are only allegations, and that each of the five accused is presumed innocent unless and until proven guilty beyond a reasonable doubt ...

(excerpted)

To all, while the temptation to focus upon the courtroom drama of the day is understandable, please also do not lose sight of the methodical movement that is taking place toward trial on the merits. Yesterday, the Judge issued a ruling on the outstanding issues associated with the classified information protective order that he signed in December (Appellate Exhibit 13 Series), which clears the way for the defense teams to sign their memoranda of understanding committing them to comply with that protective order, and enabling them to receive classified discovery materials. To date, nearly 100,000 unclassified documents have been previously provided to the defense, comprising much of our affirmative discovery obligations. This progress in discovery is only one of many reminders that only a fraction of complex capital litigation occurs during courtroom proceedings.

To date, the parties have briefed over 84 motions and have argued 23 motions, and the Judge has ruled on more than 25 motions. Another five motions have been withdrawn, and some nine further motions have been mooted or dismissed as moot.

# Alleged Intrusion Into Attorney-Client Discussions in the Courtroom and Elsewhere

On the 28th of January, the audio and visual transmission from the courtroom was briefly interrupted.

David Nevin, defense attorney for 9/11 mastermind Khalid Sheikh Mohammad, requests the court convene for the day so that they can question witnesses. To the left, this Pentagon security officer has the power to press a button to cut audio and produce white noise to keep sensitive information secret during court sessions. When he does, the red light next to him lights up and spins. We learned there is someone other than him, outside of court, who also has the ability to cut sound.

BOTTOM: Alleged 9/11 mastermind Khalid Sheikh Mohammed was brought to court with a four-guard escort walking beside him. He was holding what appears to be a Quran and some other documents.

After just one week's break, the 9/11 pre-trial hearings reconvened Feb. 11, 2013.

Khalid Sheikh Mohammed conferred with defense Army Cpt. Jason Wright after hearings convened for the day.

115

9-11 PRETRIAL HEARINGS MAURICE ELKINS TESTIFYING RE: COURT AUDIO SYSTEM

OPPOSITE: Feb. 12, 2013. Khalid Sheikh Mohammed, Walid bin Attash, and Ramzi Bin al Shibh sat with their defense teams. At the witness stand, Director of Courtroom Technology Maurice Elkins answered questions posed by civilian Pentagon defense lawyer James Connell III.

TOP: Khalid Sheikh Mohammed studies court documents while conferring with his defense.

BOTTOM LEFT: Army Reserves Lt. Col. Ramon Torres testified about his former duty, which was going through detainees' mail.

BOTTOM RIGHT: Navy Capt. Thomas Welsh, promoted from his last appearance as a commander, gave testimony.

TOP LEFT: Feb. 12, 2013. Khalid Sheikh Mohammed conferred with a female member of the defense team. She was dressed in modest Muslim attire in deference to the detainee's cultural customs.

TOP RIGHT: Maurice Elkins, Director of Courtroom Technology in Guantanamo, testified about the audio system when defense lawyers explored the possibility that someone outside the court could eavesdrop on their conversations.

BOTTOM LEFT: Feb. 13, 2013. Navy Lt. Alexander Homme, who worked as a lawyer at the detention center's staff attorney's office, testified via video feed from Corpus Christi Naval Station in Texas.

BOTTOM RIGHT: Navy Lt. Cmdr. George Massucco, a detention center lawyer, testified that all five detainees chose not to attend that day's hearing.

TOP LEFT: Feb. 13, 2013. Robin Maher, Director of the Death Penalty Representation Project at the American Bar Association (ABA), testified on the ABA death penalty guidelines.

TOP RIGHT: Army Col. John Bogdan, the commander of Guantanamo's detention center guard force, testified.

BOTTOM: Feb. 14, 2013. Walid bin Attash stood and, addressing the court via a translator, said that he was upset that personal belongings had been searched while he was in court. He refused to sit until he felt his concerns had been acknowledged. His defense attorney Cheryl Bormann was at the podium.

2-14-13    VICTIM FAMILY MEMBERS OBSERVE    9/11 pretrial hearings

ADML BRUCE McDONALD testifies via
video to CMDR. WALTER RUIZ, defense counsel

KSM WRITING
DURING HEARING

9/11 PRETRIAL 2-14-13

OPPOSITE: Family members of 9/11 victims watched the pre-trial hearings while Navy Cmdr. Walter Ruiz, a defense attorney, questioned retired Vice Adm. Bruce MacDonald, the Convening Authority for Military Commissions, who testified via a video link from his headquarters in Washington, D.C.

LEFT: KSM was very involved — reading and taking notes the entire time — during the hearings.

122 RIGHT: The court took a break so that the five detainees could pray. They all stood up, unrolled their prayer rugs and set them down, then commenced praying while guards stood a short distance away.

OPPOSITE: Defense attorney Cheryl Bormann questions the assistant to the Staff Judge Advocate, Lt. Cmdr. Massucco, regarding mail inspection issues; the detainees' mail had been searched while they were in court.

DEFENSE ATT'Y CHERYL BORMANN
9/11 pretrial hearings

DETAINEES MAIL INSPECTION ISSUE (SMP)
LT (CMDR) MATASSUCCO   2-14-13
ASS'T STAFF JUDGE ADVOCATE

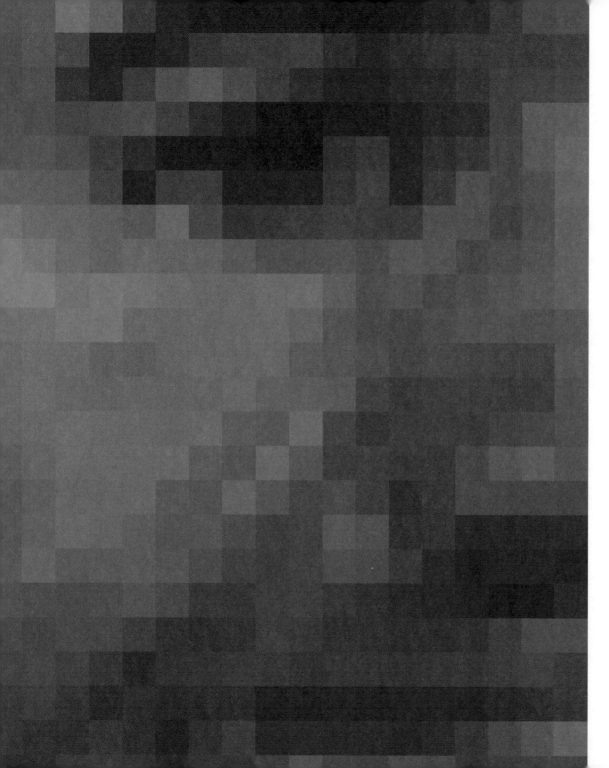

## AL NASHIRI
### Alleged U.S.S. Cole Bomber

Nov. 9, 2011. Abd al Rahim al Nashiri is seen here during his arraignment on charges of murder and terrorism, as well as other al-Qaida crimes, for allegedly setting up the suicide bombing of the U.S.S. Cole warship off Yemen, which killed 17 U.S. sailors on Oct. 12, 2000.

Al Nashiri, who said he wanted to work with both his civilian and military attorneys, did not enter a plea. In the military, the plea comes on the eve of jury selection, and pre-trial hearings handled by the judge come first. He followed the proceedings through an interpreter.

Al Nashiri's case was being closely watched. His was the first new case to move forward under President Obama, who shut down the Bush administration's tribunals in one of his first acts after taking office.

He is also the first "high-value" detainee — a senior terrorism suspect who was held for a time by the CIA at a "black site" prison and subjected to what the agency called "enhanced interrogation techniques" — to receive a trial at Guantanamo. For that reason, his case is also seen as a forerunner to the planned prosecution of Khalid Sheikh Mohammed and the other four accused conspirators in the Sept. 11 attacks.

In addition to being waterboarded, al Nashiri was subjected to mock executions when CIA operatives held a power drill and a gun to his head. Justice Department lawyers sanctioned the waterboarding, but the use of the drill and the gun fell outside interrogation techniques approved during the George W. Bush administration.

NASHIRI ARRAIGNMENT          11-9-11
Guantanamo

Navy Lt. Cmdr. Stephen Reyes questioned Navy Cmdr. Thomas Welsh, the detention center's senior staff attorney, who described how detainee documents are placed in one of two bins within their cells. One bin is intended for "legal documents," which includes anything related to the detainee's case. The other bin is for all other documents. Navy Lt. Cmdr. Reyes argued that the review involved security personnel and linguists from the prison's intelligence department "reading" all documents found within the cell, including those documents that had been placed in al Nashiri's "legal bin." Reyes contended that this review violated the attorney-client privilege.

Navy Cmdr. Andrea Lockhart took up the government's position. She argued that this one-time "baseline review" of all documents found within the detainees' cells was justified as an exercise of the detention center commander's inherent authority to run his detention facility in a manner that ensures national security, safety, and force protection. She argued those concerns outweigh the protections offered by the attorney-client privilege. Lockhart — and Cmdr. Welsh during his testimony — stated that the review did not involve "reading" the detainees' documents, but "scanning" them to determine if they were appropriately marked as attorney-client privileged communications. Although lead prosecutor Anthony Mattivi originally submitted a trial date of Feb. 2, 2012, Kammen stated that the defense would need a delay of at least a year. Mattivi did not object, provided that this constituted a "hard and fast" waiver of section 707, which relates to speedy trial rights, and Kammen stated that it did. Judge Pohl then set the trial date for Nov. 9, 2012, a date that would pass with arguments over the attorney-client privilege continuing into the next year.

VICTIM FAMILIES OBSERVE NASHIRI
ARRAIGNMENT · 11-9-11

John clodfelter
Shalala Wood

Indianapolis attorney Richard Kammen is a civilian lawyer paid by the Pentagon to defend al Nashiri. Pre-trial hearings continue as the case moves forward to eventual trial.

# MAJID KHAN

In a secret deal that delayed his sentencing hearing until 2016 in exchange for possibly testifying in the 9/11 case, Majid Khan agreed to plead guilty to plotting with KSM and working with al-Qaida by delivering $50,000 to finance blowing up a Marriott hotel in Jakarta, which killed 11 people and wounded many more.

## A Four-Hour Sit-In

After the court session, the security officer brought my sketches to Khan's lawyers for approval. The man who had just admitted to al-Qaida crimes was sitting there, and was clearly upset to see himself in a drawing. He didn't want them released. This was a first: Never before had a detainee totally stopped the release of his sketch. The court officer took them to a separate room and would not budge, even when I pointed out that if this was allowed, what would stop other detainees, maybe KSM, from preventing the public from seeing certain sketches?

The only thing I could think to do was to refuse to leave until I could talk to someone with authority. So I basically did a sit-in. The court officer was getting nervous, so he stuck around too. An hour passed, and Khan's lawyers finally came out. "Sorry," said one. "But we don't have a dog in this fight. Khan's tired and upset. Give him 24 hours and maybe he'll change his mind." Then they left.

To me, 24 hours was unthinkable. This was the only visual record of this historic guilty plea, and so I asked to make a phone call. The guards — ever polite but, well, guarded — called down to the media center. I asked to speak with our public affairs officer at the time, Navy Cmdr. Tamsen Reese.

Once she heard what was happening, she dashed over to the courtroom. By then two hours had passed. Right away she worked the phones trying to get the judge, only to get his assistant, who replied, "I don't have a dog in this fight." It seemed to be the phrase of the day. While this was going on, some guards at the court holding room with me were surfing the Web in search of rule that let a detainee censor his sketch. None could be found.

Reese and some other staff members were finally able to reach someone at the Pentagon. By then, the public affairs officer appeared nervous. She knew the military was about to hold a press conference. Nobody wanted the story of the day to be that a convict had censored his own sketch.

Finally, in the fourth hour of my sit-in, there was a knock at the door and someone spoke to the court security officer. He gave me my sketches within minutes, as though there had never been a problem. I rushed them over to the media center, and was met by applause from the waiting reporters, which was pretty cool. My drawings went out to the TV and news services just in time to accompany the news.

Talk about stress.

MAJID KHAN PLEADING GUILTY 2-29-12

MAJID KHAN
2·29·12

132

Majid Khan was with two of his lawyers — Wells Dixon of the Center for Constitutional Rights and Katya Jestin of Jenner & Block — when he was served with military commission charges on Monday morning. "Majid is doing well considering these challenging circumstances," they said in a statement.

Khan's military defense attorney Army Lt. Col. Jon Jackson, who is standing next to Khan here, declined to comment.

The 32-year-old Pakistani native pleaded guilty to war crimes for joining the terror organization after the Sept. 11 attacks and moving $50,000 used to fund a 2003 terrorist bombing of a Marriott hotel in Southeast Asia. He also admitted to conspiring with the self-proclaimed 9/11 mastermind, Khalid Sheikh Mohammed, to blow up fuel tanks and poison water supplies in the United States, and to assassinate former Pakistani President Pervez Musharraf. Neither plot was realized.

But under a plea deal, he agreed to testify at future war crimes trials and postpone his sentencing until 2016, with hopes of eventual freedom.

134    Family members of U.S.S. Cole victims watched the arraign-
       ment. I ran out of time and was unable to finish this sketch
       in color; once a drawing is approved and court is convened,
       I stop working on the art, other than cleanup.

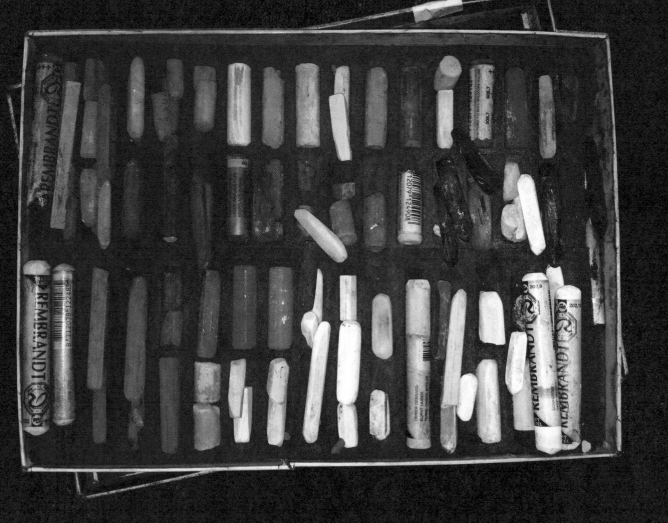

# FROM THE OUTSIDE IN

Sketchbook and Photos

GTMO at DUSK
9/5/06
ps. got adrenaline

*outside the media center* 3/25/07

LOT

parking lot

OPPOSITE: Here's a walk toward the 139
beach. You cannot see it, but there are
underground bunkers everywhere.

LEFT: We worked out of different media
centers over the years. Outside this
one, you can see the building contain-
ing Courtroom 1 in the background.

140    The former Camp X-Ray is now
       abandoned and overgrown. It was the
       first holding area for detainees, and
       the place where the infamous scenes
       of hooded and shackled detainees in
       orange jumpsuits were photographed.

2 may sunday Camp X-RAy

Camp X-Ray @ Gitmo          2-May 2010

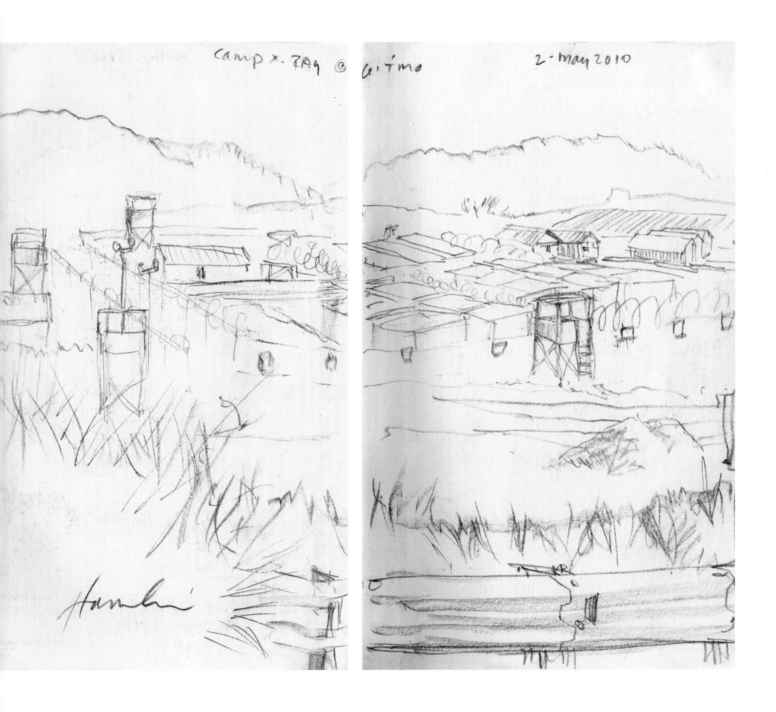

142 RIGHT: Army Lt. Col. Jon Jackson, here serving as a military defense lawyer for Canadian Omar Khadr, meets with reporters inside the McCalla Hangar, near the media center.

OPPOSITE: An earlier media workspace from another angle: Now that Camp Justice is built, McCalla Hangar has become media central.

OUTSIDE THE MEDIA AREA.

COMNAVBASE
GUANTANAMO BAY

went to the courtroom after lunch.
can't draw that 2d3 or theme behind it.

144

TOP LEFT: TV media had covered areas for their equipment, with remote satellite links, in 2007. Now they use direct links and more sheltered areas by McCalla Hangar.

BOTTOM LEFT: A sculpture sits outside the detention center hospital, overlooking the ocean. Green mesh netting prevents detainees from seeing either the sculpture or the ocean.

RIGHT: April, 2006. Court docket notes.

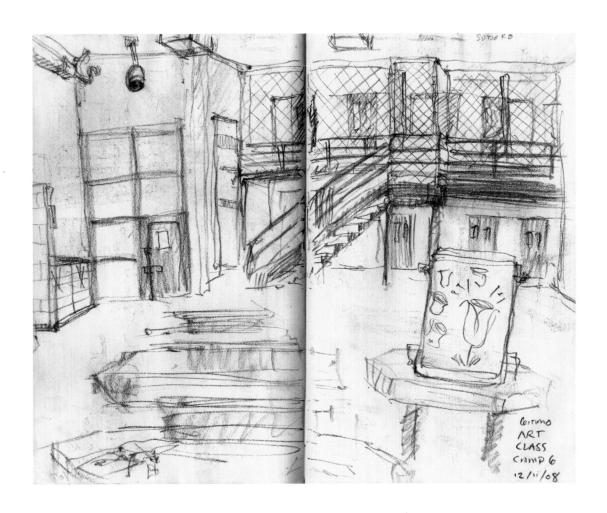

Among the many classes provided for detainees are art lessons. Students are given drawing pads and supplies. The lesson on display was how to draw a simple, Disney-like rose.

145

RIGHT: During a break while covering the Khadr hearings, we got a tour of the camps. The troops had imposed tougher rules on the media, so I submitted my sketches to a security review, just in case.

OPPOSITE LEFT: At the detention center hospital, we saw hospital beds inside cells, which made it clear this is a prison.

OPPOSITE RIGHT: We could see the detainees through one-way glass. Here they cheer at a soccer game on a mounted TV in a communal area.

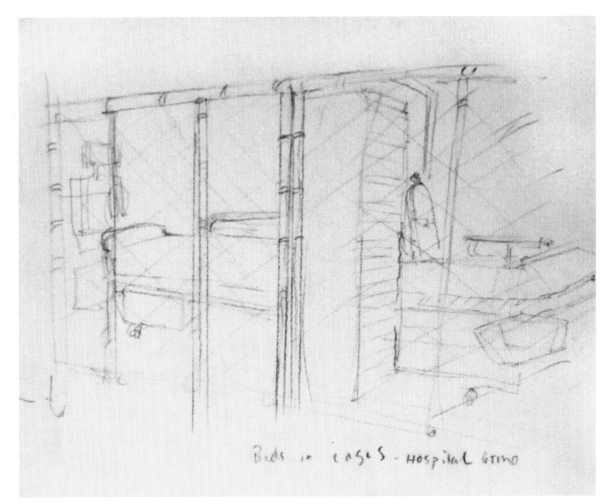

Beds in cases - Hospital GTMO

watching TV - Soccer game inside camp
4-22-10

Hank.

148   LEFT: Detainees who are on a hunger strike are shackled to this restraint chair during force-feeding.

RIGHT: A doctor displayed tubes and liquid nutrition given to those on the hunger strike. Butter Pecan was the favored flavor, a doctor said, because they can taste it when they burp.

Force
feeding chair
in a back cell

DR. Describing feeding tube procedure    10/23/10

ENTERING CAMP FOR TOUR

TOUR W/ HAYHURST          MAY 31, 2009

An entrance to one of the camps.          149

LEFT: Inside Camp 5 there are white acoustic ceilings to mute sound. Detainees get food through a feeding-tray opening, and sometimes toss what are referred to as "bodily fluid cocktails." You can see it splattered on the white ceiling. Eyewash stations are all around.

RIGHT: Some cells have tall, thin windows with metal mesh inside glass. In this case, the view was to fences upon fences.

OPPOSITE: Once inside, layers of fences segregate captives from guards and separate different portions of the camp. The military lets detainees cultivate plants in box planters.

150

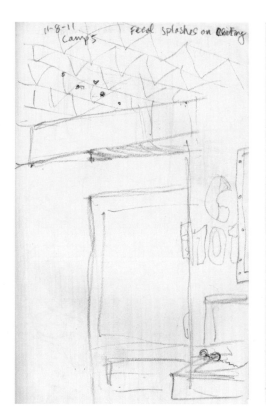

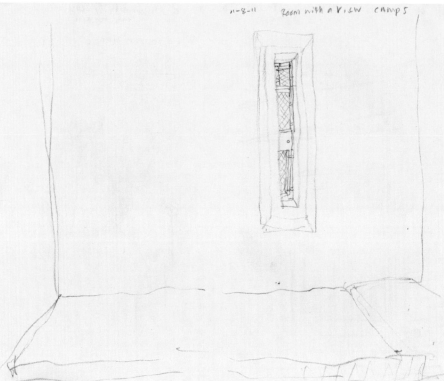

"INSIDE TRACK"

Fences inside Fences

GITMO
4-27-10

TOP LEFT: Detainees taking language lessons in a camp communal space within the camp: I keep features deliberately vague. We are not allowed to photograph or sketch any facial features in the camps.

TOP RIGHT: Sometimes the most mundane things become big deals. In this case, we were shown a soccer field being constructed for cooperative detainees, and we were told it would cost about $744,000 to build. Congress and others reacted with fury to the reported expense, so the Pentagon forbade reporters to see the prison camps while at Guantanamo to report on military commissions.

BOTTOM LEFT: A press meeting during the May 2010 Khadr hearings: NBC correspondent Shawna Thomas in the foreground, taping. To the left, in front, is Al-Arabiya's Muna Shikaki.

BOTTOM RIGHT: Army Brig. Gen. Mark Martins meets with the press in a roundtable discussion. A Rhodes scholar and graduate of Harvard Law School, he is a Chief Prosecutor of Military Commissions.

OPPOSITE: Army Brig. Gen. Mark Martins at another roundtable meeting. From left to right: Carol Rosenberg of *The Miami Herald*, Army Lt. Col. Todd Breasseale — the Pentagon spokesman responsible for Guantanamo and legal issues — Martins, and the Associated Press's Ben Fox.

152

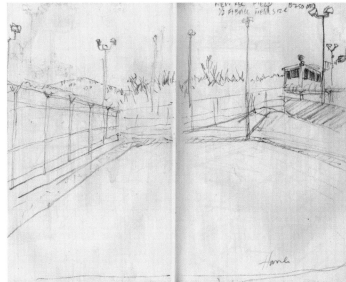

154

TOP LEFT: Camp X-Ray today. Nature has taken over: branches have entwined the cages that served as cells.

TOP RIGHT: Guard towers, fencing, and coiled wire border the perimeters of the now-abandoned Camp X-Ray.

BOTTOM LEFT: An unusual flower grew in the ruins.

BOTTOM CENTER AND RIGHT: Many trees like this grow in Guantanamo. If you open the pod, you'll find a seed shaped like a fish with scales inside.

I ABSENT: GENDER, RANK, SERVICE NOT DISCLOSED

AF COL 2 ~~GULF WAR~~ TORNADO PILOT; 3 KIDS

ARMY LTC 3 03 IRAQ WAR VET, READ ~~LOOKING TOWER TOOK~~ 3, 10-YO KIDS ~~SHOOTING~~

ARMY COL 4 ~~LOST TROOPS~~ TO IED 04 BAGHDAD, WAS BATTALION COR ~~READ~~

NAVY CAPT 5 ~~GTMO~~ TODAY "KINDA, QUESTION" NO-WIN SITUATION, POLITICAL/INTERNATIONAL PROBLEM

MARINE COL 6 7 PURPLE HEART, WOUNDED WHILE LOST IN 03 IRAQ, STUMBLED INTO FIREFIGHT

7 ABSENT: GENDER, RANK, SERVICE NOT DISCLOSED

ARMY LTC 8 15 MONTHS AS HEALTH ADMIN IN DETENTION CENTER
LOST GOOD WALTER REED FRIEND IN PENTAGON ON 9/11

NAVY CDR 9

ARMY LTC 10 ♀ cx MP SERVED IN HAITI, WAS PICKED UP PADDY WAGONED UNDERAGE DRINKING IN COLLEGE

AF LTC 11 ♀ ~~EER GTMO GUARD~~, LOST ACADEMY FRIEND TO AFGH IED ATTACK

NAVY CDR 12 SUBMARINER

ARMY MAJ 13 ♀ FRIEND'S HUBBY HURT IN IRAQ IED ATTACK

AF CPT 14 MI CONTROLLER ~~DAD WAS SVET AF POW~~, DOESN'T READ PAPERS

AF CPT 15 ~~SUBORD H.T OY 12~~ JUVENILES RESPONSIBLE ~~NF~~ ♂, ~~POLICE~~ ~~WITH THIS GUY~~

ARMY LTC 16 CLOSE GTMO GUARD, cx ARMS CONTROL ACADEMIC 2 YRS
NOT SURE DON'T WAR CRIMES CHARGES LEGITIMATE

AF COL 17 CAMP CROPPER IRAQ 07
STUCK W/ CW, QUESTIONED IN CLOSED
SESSION THAT EXCLUDED KHADR + MEDIA ok

06 = COL OR NAVY CAPT
05 = LTCOL OR NAVY CDR
04 = MAJ OR LCDR
03 = CPT OR NAVY LT

= PROSECUTION OBJECTED

= DEFENSE OBJECTS

TOP: Some people call *The Miami Herald*'s Carol Rosenberg "The Dean" because she has covered Guantanamo since the detainees first arrived, and makes sure everything runs smoothly. She kept a whiteboard updated with fact-checked, correct information for the rest of the media. Seen here: Notes on the Khadr jury during its selection process.

With a constant rotation of military support staff every six to 12 months, it helps to have returning Guantanamo reporters help out the new arrivals.

BOTTOM: Two places at one time: The American Forces Network broadcast a PBS interview with Carol Rosenberg, filmed minutes before outside the media room. From left: *Los Angeles Times* reporter Carol Williams, and the *Toronto Star*'s Michelle Shephard.

155

156

This view is from a balcony inside
the McCalla Hangar, where all things
media happen — from the workroom
behind the brown door to live video
shots along the perimeter out front. The
small air-conditioned building built for
press and media is now used primarily
for security reviews of film and instruc-
tional purposes.

TOP LEFT: A mini-commissary and food-vending van is sometimes available for meal purchases under the "Search and Rescue" sign. The store didn't last long, so we now primarily depend on shuttles to fast food outlets on base, or group grocery shopping from the main commissary. The military has set up a cafeteria near our work-space, but members of the media are forbidden from using it.

Occasionally a food truck will drive up with sandwiches, hot dogs, fruit cups, and coffee.

TOP CENTER: Fast food restaurants Subway and McDonald's exist in Guantanamo.

TOP RIGHT: Sketches are posted up for live shots outside the workspace.

BOTTOM: Sketches are posted outside the reporters' filing center for paying TV crews to film.

158

TOP: Inside the media's workspace: To the left, military minders are present 24/7 to assist and oversee. The media work at desks equipped with $150-a-week Ethernet cables. The military posts troops in the room around the clock. A monitor on the wall lets reporters write and tweet court activities real time. One designated reporter provides inside-court details that the monitors don't show.

BOTTOM: A press conference was held after Khadr's trial, with Speer's widow and the prosecution.

OPPOSITE: Walking to court. That's me out front with my board and supplies. To the right, in uniform, is now-retired Navy Cmdr. J.D. Gordon, the officer who was my escort when KSM insisted on a nose job. Carol Rosenberg is behind us. Photo courtesy AP/Brennan Linsley.

Camp Justice is where we live and work. For years, my home away from home was tent C-19, or "Charlie 19" as the *Toronto Star*'s Michelle Shephard called it.

Four or five of us would share it as regular roommates, until the military tore it down and moved us to A-11. With such little privacy, knowing your tent mates really makes a difference.

The tents have huge, windy chillers to reduce mold and to discourage the mosquito, banana rat, scorpion, crab, and snake populations.

There's a laundry tent, a shower tent, and a toilet tent. The prison staff set up a "recreation tent" specifically to segregate the reporters. Orange barricades separate the reporters from Air Force maintenance troops, who call themselves "The Beef."

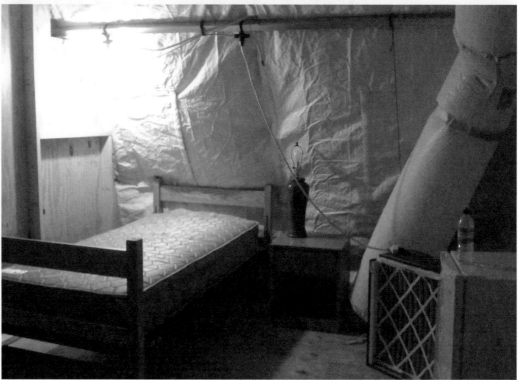

TOP LEFT: I was jogging when I first spotted these warning signs. Needless to say, I avoided that road.

TOP RIGHT: An abandoned playground, from the years when military families were housed on Guantanamo's Leeward side, looked apocalyptic.

CENTER LEFT: A podium made to look like a miniature guard tower at the airport in Gitmo.

CENTER RIGHT: Don't mess with the iguanas; there's a $10,000 fine for harming one.

BOTTOM: An elusive banana rat: Very shy, they generally only come out at night. Our tents are kept very cold, in part to keep the rats out.

Abandoned Youngstown Girl Scout camp: now a beach
getaway.

During a day off from court we were offered a tour of
Camp Iguana, where a group of Muslims from China —
known as Uighurs — were being held. They were awaiting
a court-ordered release, but no one wanted them in the U.S.
They were fearful of returning to China and were stuck in a
kind of limbo while the U.S. Government looked for a country willing to take them. They were not allowed to talk to
the media directly, so instead they used their art supplies to
write messages on drawing paper. Suddenly a benign tour
turned into a silent protest. Within weeks, several Uighurs
were transported to Bermuda.

164

TOP LEFT: During a prison camp visit, I spotted this quilted "suicide smock" in a cell; detainees at risk of "self-harm" are issued this to wear instead of a uniform.

TOP RIGHT: Basic toilet and sink in a typical cell.

BOTTOM LEFT: Visiting units have left their mark on the ceiling tiles in the bar of the Officers' Club. The Criminal Investigation Task Force (CITF), the organization that investigates captives, put this one there.

BOTTOM RIGHT: During this visit, the military displayed the items that compliant detainees get: toilet paper, no-handle plastic razors, and other personal care items. A variety of footwear and prayer rugs are provided as well.

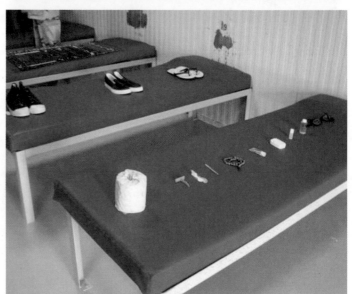

Uighurs hold signs drawn with art supplies. Another sign said, "We need to freedom."

A panoramic view from inside McCalla Hangar, known as the "Media Operations Center," with office space for reporters to hook up their computers, a shed built inside for press briefings, and the place where military censors review photography to decide what can leave Guantanamo.

Carol Rosenberg is walking past the print media workspace, which is behind the beige door.

OPSEC stands for Operational Security. Here's what the military sometimes censors:
- Faces of personnel, unless they are our escorts or specifically approved.
- Certain buildings, such as Courtroom 2, the high security court built specifically for the 9/11 co-conspirators trial.
- Orange barricades.
- More than three tents at Camp Justice.
- Waterfront shots that might give away locations.
- What the fence-line with Cuba looks like.
- Satellite or communications devices.

# AFTERWORD

by Karen J. Greenberg

Guantanamo. It has been in the news constantly for more than a decade. It is the place where as many as 779 detainees were held in the decade after 9/11: the focal point for the innumerable controversies that have surrounded the American response to terrorism — from protests over U.S. detention policies and interrogation techniques, to pragmatic and philosophical concerns over the viability of military commissions, to diplomatic relations with the detainees' countries of origin. The issues that coalesce at Guantanamo are symbolic of the range of moral, legal, and policy questions that have persisted throughout the ongoing War on Terror.

Despite the vastness of the problems represented by Guantanamo and the persistence of Guantanamo-related stories in the press, there have been very few images of Guantanamo Bay Detention Facility, a camp that opened four months after 9/11 and has existed for more than 11 years. The U.S. government has kept a tight hold on any photographic images coming out of the detention facility. Photographs and drawings are carefully scrutinized and cleared by military personnel on the grounds of protecting national security — ostensibly out of respect for the detainees' right not to be photographed. The absence of imagery has contributed to the dehumanization of the detainees. In place of faces, the American public has witnessed abstract policy debates. In place of the stories that pictures can convey, the public has been handed carefully controlled official narratives.

The military commissions have given us a chance to see more, as sketch artists have been allowed — albeit with great restrictions — to document the proceedings. Janet Hamlin characterizes her work as "visual journalism"; Lt. Col. Jackson refers to her as a "visual historian." She is both. Here, in this special volume, Hamlin invites the public — and posterity — to peer into the personalities and lives that have filled the courtrooms at Guantanamo Bay. Here, in her drawings, we can witness not just the detainees but also the entire community that has grown up around the military commissions — the lawyers, journalists, victims' families, personnel, and the detainees themselves.

The military commissions have traveled a bumpy road since their inception, and have had numerous iterations. Formally, the military commissions process began in 2006 after the passage of the Military Commissions Act (MCA). Congress passed this initial MCA in response to the Supreme Court ruling that President George W. Bush did not have the authority to establish the military tribunals that had been set up at Guantanamo; rather, such a system of military commissions

needed to be authorized by Congress. Under the MCA, three detainees were found guilty — Australian David Hicks and two Yemenis, Salim Hamdan and al Hamza al Bahlul. Despite their convictions, the military commissions process was seen by many critics as a poor form of justice, lacking transparency, proper evidentiary standards, and reliable procedural consistency. Incorporating these criticisms, Congress passed a new Military Commissions Act under President Barack Obama. Under the 2009 version of the Military Commissions Act, there have been four convictions, that of two Sudanese — Ibrahim Ahmed Mahmoud al Qosi and Noor Uthman Mohammed — as well as the young Canadian Omar Khadr and the Pakistani Majid Khan. In addition, five individuals, including the alleged mastermind of 9/11, Khalid Sheikh Mohammed, are now in pre-trial hearings for the 9/11 attacks, as is Abd al Rahim al Nashiri for the U.S.S. Cole bombing.

But despite the steam the commissions seemed to pick up under the Obama administration, the process has sputtered continually, suffering serious setbacks. Of the initial convictions, two have been overturned. Meanwhile, the trials of the 9/11 defendants have encountered obstacle after obstacle. Hamlin has captured this well in her drawings detailing the arraignment of these defendants, a process which is usually extremely quick but which, in the military commissions court, went late into the night, ending after 13 hours. Pre-trial hearings and controversial issues have delayed the start of the 9/11 trial, which is now unlikely to begin before 2014.

These sketches bring to life the human drama that has accompanied the commissions from the start. Despite the harsh rules the media must follow and constant oversight of sketches, these pictures give us startling glimpses into the world of the military commissions. From these drawings, we can see not only the individual players but also the relationships between them. We see the bewilderment and sadness of Omar Khadr, who spent 10 of his 26 years at Guantanamo and who is seen here sitting shoulder-to-shoulder with his Canadian civilian defense attorney, Dennis Edney. We see the defiance of the 9/11 defendants who refuse to show up in court, leaving the families of the 9/11 victims to ponder their empty seats. We see the slight look of disdain on Judge Pohl's face as he watches defense attorney Cheryl Bormann address the court dressed in a hijab. We see the relatively large and intensely focused pool of reporters watching the trial.

On the one hand it is a thankless task to report on the Guantanamo military commissions. The reporters are scrutinized and distrusted, and their work is subject to censor and rejection. On the other hand it is an immensely worthwhile occupation. Without these images — be they from sketches or from reporting by journalists such as Carol Rosenberg and Michelle Shephard, whose essays appear in this volume — Guantanamo would have remained even less visible to the public eye, a mere policy issue, devoid of faces, personalities, and the human element that is at the center of these trials and of Guantanamo as a detention facility. Moreover, in years to come, when historians look back on the Guantanamo era, these drawings will be among the most valuable reportage that can help tell the story. Covering Guantanamo has been a long-term commitment. It will remain so until the day that it closes. Here, in these pages, the struggles and significance of that commitment are readily apparent. ★

*Karen J. Greenberg is the Director of the Center on National Security, and a noted expert on national security, terrorism, and civil liberties. She is the editor of* The Torture Debate in America *(2006), and the author of* The Least Worst Place: Guantanamo's First 100 Days *(2009), which was selected as one of the best books of 2009 by The Washington Post and Slate.com.*

Fantagraphics Books
7563 Lake City Way NE
Seattle, Washington 98115

Edited by Gary Groth and Kristy Valenti
Designed by Jacob Covey
Proofreader: Janice Lee
Editorial Assistance: Keith Barbalato, Tom Graham, Toby Liebowitz
Associate Publisher: Eric Reynolds
Published by Gary Groth

To receive a free full-color catalog of comics, graphic novels, prose novels, and collections of visual art, call 1-800-657-1100, or visit fantagraphics.com. You may order books at our web site or by phone.

ISBN: 978-1-60699-691-1

First Fantagraphics printing: October, 2013

Printed in Hong Kong